'Paul Lawrence has done it again! In this jewel of a book, he holds our hands as we get deeper and deeper into the systemic world, offering us new ideas, challenging the mindsets we didn't know we had, and pushing us to be more reflective and more expansive about our practice. Equally useful for beginning coaches and for those who have been coaching for decades, there are already a dozen people I'm going to gift a copy of this stimulating and compassionate book.'

Jennifer Garvey Berger, Chief Executive Officer, Cultivating Leadership

Coaching Systemically

This book provides an accessible and clear description of key theories of systemic coaching and how they can be applied to coaching practice.

Structured around five different ways of thinking about systems, the book provides coaches with a high-level overview of different systems theories and how those theories may be applied in practice. Readers are invited to consider each of the five different ways of thinking through the lens of philosophy, purpose and practice: Which theories most resonate for you? How do these systemic perspectives shape your purpose for coaching, and how do they show up in the way that you coach? With examples and case material throughout, *Coaching Systemically* aligns coaching with the realities and challenges of organisations operating in an ever more complex world.

Readers will walk away from the book with a clearer understanding of what it means to coach 'systemically' and new ideas as to how they can translate insights into practice. *Coaching Systemically* will be key reading for coaches in practice and in training, consultants and anyone interested in systemic approaches.

Paul Lawrence, PhD, is a director of the Centre for Coaching in Organisations (CCO). He conducts ongoing research into coaching, leadership and change. Before becoming a coach, Paul had a long corporate career, heading up businesses in Spain, Portugal, Japan and Australia.

Essential Coaching Skills and Knowledge

Series Editors: Stephen Palmer,
Averil Leimon & Gladeana McMahon

The **Essential Coaching Skills and Knowledge** series provides an accessible and lively introduction to key areas in the developing field of coaching. Each title in the series is written by leading coaches with extensive experience and has a strong practical emphasis, including illustrative vignettes, summary boxes, exercises and activities. Assuming no prior knowledge, these books will appeal to professionals in business, management, human resources, psychology, counselling and psychotherapy, as well as students and tutors of coaching and coaching psychology.

Titles in the series:

Essential Career Transition Coaching Skills
Caroline Talbott

Group and Team Coaching
The Secret Life of Groups, Second Edition
Christine Thornton

Coaching in Three Dimensions
Meeting the Challenges of a Complex World
Paul Lawrence & Allen Moore

The Heart of Coaching Supervision
Working with Reflection and Self-Care
Edited by Eve Turner and Stephen Palmer

Coaching Systemically
Five Ways of Thinking About Systems
Paul Lawrence

For more information about the series, please visit www.routledge.com/series/ECS

Coaching Systemically

Five Ways of Thinking About Systems

Paul Lawrence

Routledge
Taylor & Francis Group

LONDON AND NEW YORK

First published 2021
by Routledge
2 Park Square, Milton Park, Abingdon, Oxon OX14 4RN

and by Routledge
52 Vanderbilt Avenue, New York, NY 10017

Routledge is an imprint of the Taylor & Francis Group, an informa business

British Library Cataloguing-in-Publication Data
A catalogue record for this book is available from the British Library

Library of Congress Cataloging-in-Publication Data
Names: Lawrence, Paul, 1963– author.
Title: Coaching systemically : five ways of thinking about systems /
   Paul Lawrence.
Description: Abingdon, Oxon ; New York, NY : Routledge, 2021. | Series:
   Essential coaching skills and knowledge | Includes bibliographical
   references and index. | Summary: "This book provides an accessible and
   clear description of key theories of systemic coaching and how they
   can be applied to coaching practice. Structured around five different
   ways of thinking about systems, the book provides coaches with a high-
   level overview of different systems theories and how those theories may
   be applied in practice. Readers are invited to consider each of the five
   different ways of thinking through the lens of philosophy, purpose and
   practice: Which theories most resonate for you? How do these systemic
   perspectives shape your purpose for coaching, and how do they show up
   in the way that you coach? With examples and case material throughout,
   Coaching Systemically aligns coaching with the realities and challenges
   of organisations operating in an ever more complex world. Readers will
   walk away from the book with a clearer understanding of what it means
   to coach 'systemically' and new ideas as to how they can translate
   insights into practice. Coaching Systemically will be key reading for
   coaches in practice and in training, consultants and anyone interesting in
   systemic approaches"—Provided by publisher.
Identifiers: LCCN 2020042005 (print) | LCCN 2020042006 (ebook) |
   ISBN 9780367404147 (hardback) | ISBN 9780367404161 (paperback) |
   ISBN 9780429356001 (ebook)
Subjects: LCSH: Executive coaching. | Employees—Coaching of. | Personal
   coaching.
Classification: LCC HD30.4 .L393 2021 (print) | LCC HD30.4 (ebook) |
   DDC 658.3/124—dc23
LC record available at https://lccn.loc.gov/2020042005
LC ebook record available at https://lccn.loc.gov/2020042006

ISBN: 978-0-367-40414-7 (hbk)
ISBN: 978-0-367-40416-1 (pbk)
ISBN: 978-0-429-35600-1 (ebk)

Typeset in New Century Schoolbook
by Apex CoVantage, LLC

I think it is a central aspect of the role of the coach to explore how coach and client are together thinking about how they are thinking.

Ralph Stacey

Contents

Acknowledgements

It took about 15 months to write this book, during which time I shared the ideas at various conferences and webinars. I'd like to thank the International Centre for Coaching and Mentoring Studies at Oxford Brookes University, the University of Sydney Coaching Psychology Unit, the Graduate School of Business at Queensland University of Technology (QUT) and the Association for Coaching (AC) in Queensland for inviting me along to speak at their events. I'd also like to thank the Association for Coaching, the Association for Coaching in ACT, the Association of Coaching Supervisors, the ICF in the UK and Hong Kong, Renee and Mel at the Coaching Kool-Aid and Tara Nolan for allowing me to share these ideas through webinars and podcasts. Most especially I'd like to thank the people who attended those workshops and webinars for their patience in listening to a stream of formative ideas, and for giving me feedback.

I'd like also to thank Tatiana Bachkirova and Peter Jackson for building some of this thinking into the Oxford Brookes University Coaching Supervision Program, and Amy Miszalski, Angie Tenace, Ann Wright, Charmaine O'Brien, Edna McKelvey, Genevieve Vignes, Jayne Dunn, Kerryn Velleman, Maree McPherson, Monica Cable and Tim Sprague for being guinea pigs on the first programme to feature these materials.

I'd like to thank Gordon Spence and all the students at the Sydney Business School Master's programme for their support and challenge. I'd like to thank Michael Cavanagh, Sean O'Connor, David Lane, Jennifer Garvey-Berger and

Ralph Stacey especially for their work, which I have found to be particularly inspiring in this space, and many other authors besides.

I would like to especially thank Tatiana Bachkirova (always an inspiration), Babette Graham, Suzi Skinner, Padraig O'Sullivan, Cat Dunne and Amy Miszalski for taking the time to read whole drafts of the book, and for giving me wonderful critique. And to Angela Wright, Hermann Ditzig, Geoff Abbott and Jane Cooke-Lauder, who haven't yet read the book, but have always given me great critique anyway.

Thanks to the AC Leadership team in NSW/ACT (including my co-leader Pauline Triggiani) for managing without me much of the time while I busied myself getting the book finished, the internal coaching team at KPMG (including Emma, Sarah, Hannah and Babette), Raechel Gavin and all the leaders at Quantium, the Tribe, and Amy and Cat, my business partners at the Centre for Coaching in Organisations.

And I would most especially like to thank Ashleigh, Cameron, Callum, Charlotte and Ruth for being there as family.

And everyone else I have had a conversation with.

Foreword

In the last decade the coaching field has been highly influenced by systems and complexity theories. As a consequence, now nearly every coach calls their approach to coaching 'systemic'. This tendency is noticeable in many practitioners' books. The debates about complexity and systems have also found their way into academic literature. For example, a very well-organised discussion in the special issue 7(1) of the *International Coaching Psychology Review* in 2012 is an important marker. It was based around the target paper 'Coaching Psychology Coming of Age: The challenges we face in the messy world of complexity?' written by Michael Cavanagh and David Lane (Cavanagh & Lane, 2012). The issue included commentaries from eight well-known academics, including Ralph Stacey, whose work (Stacey, 2003) had been an inspiration for the authors of the lead paper and the foundation of their argument.

Interestingly, Stacey's contribution to this debate about the role of the coach in a complex world was clear and insightful, but it appeared minimalist to those who tend to make grand claims about their systemic approaches such as, for example, 'transforming the whole organisation'. Stacey's argument was grounded and demystifying, indicating that the most useful thing a coach can do is to engage in a reflexive exploration with their client, which can sustain and develop the client's capacity for practical judgement. He called this work the hallmark of an expert practitioner. In more specific terms he implied that "the central aspect of the role of coaching is to explore how coach and client are together thinking about how they are thinking" (Stacey, 2012: 94–95). Interestingly, this message was not picked up by wider coaching audiences. Claims about systemic and complexity approaches remained exaggerated and overpublicized without any reasonable explanation about the actual role of the coach in such approaches, until Paul Lawrence's work and publications.

The importance of Paul's work is in bringing us right back to the essence of actual coaching practice: what the coach can do in order 'to think together with the client about their thinking' and how this thinking can be improved. In doing so, he clearly demonstrates that system and complexity approaches are far from homogeneous, and some of them may not be that dissimilar to the typically criticised linear ways of interpreting systems. It becomes clear that coaches who name their approach as systemic may be working with clients, and facilitating their thinking together, at various levels of complexity. This is not surprising considering how many different ways there are of conceptualising systems and complexity. Difficult, often opaque, theories of complexity become live in this book as a consequence of being translated into the nuances and issues of real coaching work, both individually and in teams.

Although it is team coaching that is usually associated with systemic coaching, I particularly want in this foreword to bring the attention of the reader to the importance of coaching individuals in organisations. My commentary on the paper by Cavanagh and Lane in the seminal issue that I mentioned previously may have been seen as a 'wet blanket' for the hype associated with systemic approaches. It was called 'Let us not throw out the individual baby with the non-systemic bath water' (Bachkirova, 2012). I am still concerned that the main strength of coaching which I see as an individualised tailormade, rather than blanket, approach to development of people at work – can simply be sacrificed to more fashionable work with teams 'in service of organisations'.

The tendency to replace individual coaching with team coaching is noticeable in organisations and supported by coaches themselves, and I would like to offer a note of caution for some flaws in the way this movement is being justified. For example, a simple misunderstanding that can give rise to the underestimation of individual coaching is the conflation of 'individual' with 'individualistic'. It is also a gross oversimplification to think that working with more than one client at a time is more systemic or more influential for effectiveness of systems. Both can have greater or lesser degrees of utility depending on a whole range of factors. It is also worth mentioning that there is currently more evidence for the effectiveness of individual coaching than there is for team coaching. I would go as far as to say that prioritising team coaching might sometimes be a disguised intention of organisational 'strategists' to sneak in a short-term agenda of fixing organisational problems instead of the potentially longer-term developmental agenda for all employees. We know that developing individuals has no less important benefits, since individuals can change organisations in profound ways.

Getting back to the topic of systems and complexity, I would argue that the careful unpicking of the individuals' thinking about their role in local organisational conversations and the shift they can make in terms of their role in these conversations may produce a butterfly effect more significant than trying to create a synergy between individuals who are confused and lost in the dynamics of teams. A lesser practical issue is that working with teams makes coaches join a whole army of other practitioners, such as group facilitators, consultants, team-building experts, leaving them with the troublesome task of differentiating themselves from these groups. Coaching individual clients, in contrast, has a unique and very important niche with unlimited opportunities for influencing not only a client but also an organisation, because organisations consist of people.

On a more important conceptual level, I would be seriously concerned if coaches began to think that systemic approaches "are less interested in the individuals and more in the patterns of interaction between them" (Cavanagh & Lane, 2012: 78). Minimising a focus of attention in coaching in such a way is clearly another form of reductionism. If there was a sin of excluding interaction and wider contexts from the focus of some types of individual coaching, then excluding individuals is no less a sin as far as systems are concerned. Paul Lawrence does not commit such a sin. His examples take us to the realm of coaching individual clients, and he does this systemically.

Just one more thing to add in support of in-depth individual coaching. Recent developments in biology, psychology, neuroscience and sociology show how complex a human being is, let alone how we change and develop. Working with individuals on a professional level requires embracing complexity and system theories no less than working with groups and organisations. This level of complexity starts with recognition that "like the Earth's ecosystems, our boundaries are porous with energy and matter flowing continually through them, while component cells that make up our bodies are constantly recycled" (Oliver, 2020: 34). Our individual perceptions of events constantly change because of numerous situational factors, sometimes not even visibly relevant (Bermudez, 2018: 273). Our beliefs and intentions are embedded in cultures and intersubjective discourses as well as in economic and social systems that are continually in flux. Therefore, to engage properly with the complexity of individuals and their actions is quite an undertaking for a serious practitioner.

Finally, thinking systemically may look deceptively easy, but this book clearly shows that it is not just saying that you care about the whole organisation as much as your individual client. It is not even enough to say that you are an integral part of the clients' systems. In shattering such simplicity, this book may stretch your thinking to the extent that it might feel uncomfortable. However, if you are not in the business of feeling comfortable, you will have a treat working on your own development. I have been advocating the importance of 'system intelligence' for coaches after Hämäläinen and Saarinen (2008) introduced this concept. Engaging with Paul Lawrence's book is designed to increase your system intelligence by inviting you to take a close look at who you are in relation to your practice and how you work. I suggest you do not skip the theoretical part of the book. Development of system intelligence is increased when we visit and revisit a wide range of theories and conceptual perspectives. Add a significant boost to your level of reflexivity, plus a fair degree of criticality, and this becomes a good recipe for a fantastic learning.

Tatiana Bachkirova

References

Bachkirova, T. (2012). Let us not throw out the individual baby with the non-systemic bath water. *International Coaching Psychology Review*, 7(1), 98–100.

Bermudez, J. L. (2018). *The bodily self: Selected essays*. Cambridge, MA: MIT Press.

Cavanagh, M., & Lane, D. (2012). Coaching psychology coming of age: The challenges we face in the messy world of complexity? *International Coaching Psychology Review*, 7(1), 75–90.

Hämäläinen, R. P., & Saarinen, E. (2008). Systems intelligence – The way forward? A note on Ackoff's 'Why few organizations adopt systems thinking'. *Systems Research and Behavioral Science*, 25(6), 821–825.

Oliver, T. (2020). *The self-delusion: The surprising science of how we are connected and why that matters*. London: Weidenfeld & Nicolson.

Stacey, R. D. (2003). *Complexity and group processes: A radically social understanding of individuals*. Hove, UK: Brunner-Routledge.

Stacey, R. D. (2012). Comment on debate article: Coaching psychology coming of age: The challenges we face in the messy world of complexity? *International Coaching Psychology Review*, 7(1), 91–96.

Introduction

This is a book about how we think about the complexities of life. Some complexities we experience within our organisations, as leaders and coaches. This book offers perspectives as to how we might think differently about those challenges. Other complexities, such as climate change and COVID-19, we face together. In this book we'll make reference to both climate change and COVID-19 because we are all familiar with those issues. Consider climate change, for example. Rush Limbaugh, a radio personality in the USA, is reputed to have said:

> I have a theory about global warming and why people think it's real. Go back 30, 40 years when there was much less air conditioning in the country. When you didn't have air conditioning and you left the house, it may in fact have gotten a little cooler out there, because sometimes houses become hot boxes. Now, 30, 40 years later, all this air conditioning, and it's a huge difference when you go outside. When you go outside now, my golly, is it hot. Oh. Global warming. It's all about the baseline you're using for comparison.

A former world leader is quoted as saying:[1]

> Climate change itself is probably doing good; or at least more good than harm. There's the evidence that higher concentrations of carbon dioxide – which is a plant food after all – are actually greening the planet and helping to lift agricultural yields. In most countries, far more people die

in cold snaps than in heatwaves, so a gradual lift in global temperatures, especially if it's accompanied by more prosperity and more capacity to adapt to change, might even be beneficial.

Putting aside the wisdom of these arguments for a moment, consider the way each speaker appears to be thinking. Both arguments seem to be based on a belief that causality is linear and straightforward; A + B = C. People now have air conditioning, therefore they feel the heat more when they go outside, therefore they think the world is warmer. Or, the world is getting warmer, fewer people die when the weather is warmer, therefore global warming is a good thing. This linear way of thinking is often useful. For example, if I am cold and I put my heater on, I will be warmer. But sometimes linear rationality leads us to make bad decisions because the relationship between cause and effect is not always linear. In seeking to manage the impact of climate change, we need to think outside the linear. Instead we see people espousing different linear theories engaging in debate as to which linear theory is right and which is wrong.

Writing more than half a century ago, Gregory Bateson (anthropologist, social scientist, ecologist) said that purposeful, pragmatic action usually results in disaster because we constantly overestimate our capacity to understand the world around us.[2] Conscious purpose contributes to the escalation of conflict as different purposes collide. Yet society values conscious purpose and idealises authoritative leadership. Bateson was writing 50 years ago, yet his concerns resonate even more today. We still fail in our attempts to navigate complexity. In responding to climate change, Brexit, COVID-19, conflict between nations, we see time and again people attempting to reduce complexity to single, simple causal connections. Simple causal explanations enable us to feel we are in control. Working off these explanations, we put together action plans. When those plans don't work, we make up reasons, based on new simple causal explanations. All the time, we criticise others for being unable to prove their different simple causal explanations.

If this is a big problem for us as a global community, then what are coaches doing about it? I would argue that many of us are exacerbating the problem. We tell ourselves our clients have the answer, that the answer lies within. We encourage them to move quickly to identify a goal, build plans and take action. We hold them to account, making sure they follow through on agreed commitments. And as the world gets busier and more complex, so we oblige in helping our clients to solve problems faster, to implement solutions without asking questions, all in service of getting things done. At the heart of this problem lies our reluctance to slow down and reflect upon the complexity of our environment. To think about events differently. If our clients need to make time to think differently, then coaches need to role model that behaviour. It is not our role to tell our clients what to do. It is not our role to hold our clients to account to our agendas. But it is our role to learn to think differently and to further develop our capacity to challenge our clients to think differently. In response to the world becoming more complex, we hear more often the clarion call. For example:[3]

> The crises we face are systemic in nature. To overcome those crises, we need to understand how systems work. To arrive at such an understanding, we need to think systemically.

Notice the call to 'understand how systems work'. To think systemically not only entails taking a broader view, it means also building our understanding of what we see. To step back and observe everyone in an organisation rushing around, attending meetings, having ad-hoc conversations, enables us to see things holistically. But what is going on? How should we interpret the unfurling of events? What sense do we make of it all? What sense we make of events depends on the lens through which we view those events. To say we view things holistically is one thing, but to say we views things systemically implies we have a working theory of systems and how they operate.

The only aspect of 'systemically' that everyone currently agrees upon is that it means to take a broader view. Nevertheless, the rush is already on to copyright and own terms such as 'systemic coaching' in service of marketing new tools and development offerings. These tools and approaches often have minimal theoretical underpinnings or context. We in the coaching community appear determined to repeat the events of 25 years ago in the systems dynamics community:[4]

> Using the term 'systems thinking' in a way which is both imprecise and, apparently, unaware of intellectual antecedents . . . has the effect of blurring the boundaries between different approaches. The employment of this term to describe our own single methodology is virtually to deny the existence of any other, if we use that term for our own discipline, we are putting ourselves in a mental prison.

We are a commercial community, and there is a danger that we tread the same path in exploring systems thinking as we did in exploring neuroscience. As Professor Anthony Grant, renowned coaching psychologist, once said about 'neuro-leadership':

> . . . neuroscience-based coaching is a classic example of pop-science band-wagoning with coaches, workplace trainers and business consultants using neuroscientific jargon and brain images as pseudo-explanatory frameworks for atheoretical proprietary coaching systems.

It falls on us all to learn from each other and collaborate in teaching ourselves what it means to think more systemically. The task begins with acknowledging the depth and breadth of understanding that exists already outside our community.

In the coaching supervision world, the seven-eyed model is popular (Figure I.1).[5] It prompts coach and supervisor to think beyond the two-way relationship between coach and coachee. This is useful because it prompts us to notice the role that others are playing in the coach's predicament. But that is all it does. It doesn't offer any insights as to the way the broader 'system' operates, what to look out for or how to navigate that 'system'.

Peter Hawkins, one of the authors of the model, has already suggested that coaching supervisors be trained in

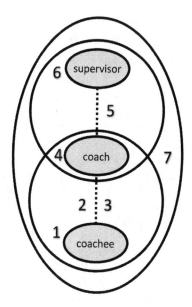

Figure I.1 Seven-eyed model of coaching supervision
Source: Hawkins & Smith (2006)

systemic thinking. The danger is that just as a plethora of neuro-coaching schools have proliferated over the last few years, so will there sprout a similar proliferation of systemic coaching schools, too many promoting proprietary models and frameworks based on fuzzy theoretical underpinnings. As Hawkins suggests, the answer must be for us all to take responsibility for developing our own personal 'epistemologies', or knowledge bases.[6] In other words, we need to educate ourselves. We need to stand back and ask ourselves what different people appear to mean when they use phrases like 'systems thinking' and 'systemic'. We need to challenge their models and frameworks in service of deciding for ourselves what meanings most resonate.

The way you operate as a coach is based on how you think about the world, and about change and how change works. The way you operate is based on the theoretical lens you choose to look through. We all have a lens, and we all make implicit assumptions about how the world around us operates. Many of us are unaware what lens it is we look through and are unaware that other lenses exist. If we are to help our clients address the issues of today, then we must be inquisitive and committed to learn. As we learn we access new perspectives, through which we can scrutinize our own dearly held assumptions and the confident assertions of others.

This is a journey that extends well beyond the world of coaching competencies.[7] Many coaching schools and industry associations tell us that to become a coach is to learn a set of skills. This is to compare coaching to carpentry. So long as I have a full bag of good tools and an understanding as to how I should use those tools, I will be a good coach. Whatever the scenario, whosoever the client, the answer always sits in my bag of tools. Scenario A requires me to deploy competencies four and six. Scenario B requires me to deploy competencies one, two, nine and twelve. Deploying the right set of competencies will deliver the desired outcome. This is first order thinking as described in Chapters 2 and 3, and if we don't collectively find insights and wisdom beyond first order systems thinking, we may continue to support destruction and disorder – without knowing it.

The book

In its broadest sense, to be *systemic* simply means 'relating to or involving a whole system'[8] and the word *system* means only 'a set of elements standing in interrelation among themselves and with the environment'.[9] Therefore, to be a systemic coach means only that you pay attention to what's happening in the broader environment rather than focus too narrowly on the presenting issue. To be systemic says nothing about how you think systems work. There are lots of different systems theories, all of which depict the system differently, and each of which has something to offer in encouraging us to think about our clients' issues in a new way. The problem is that many of these systems theories are not easy to understand, nor is it easy to see how these theories might apply in a practical sense. The purpose of this book is to bring an essence of these theories to life in a way that enables coaches to become more aware of the way they currently think and how their quality of thinking impacts on those they work with.

Five versions of systemic

Rather than proceed theory by theory, the book is structured around five broad categories of theory (Figure I.2). Key distinctions between these categories are highlighted in terms of theory and coach attitudes and behaviours. Descriptions of these theories are deliberately kept high-level and broad, but if you'd like to explore any of these theories in greater depth, then the book provides guidance as to where to look.

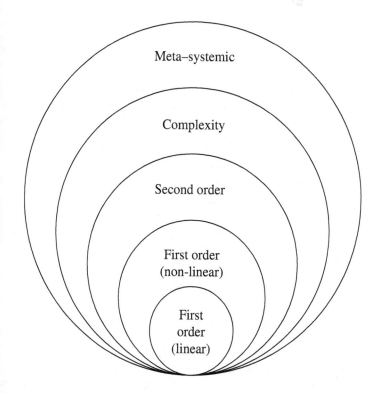

Meta–systemic

Complexity

Second order

First order
(non-linear)

First
order
(linear)

Figure I.2 Five ways of thinking about systems

The five categories, in short, are:

1 First order – linear thinking
Coach and leader see organisations as real systems. Every system can be broken down into its constituent parts, and the relationships between parts are relatively easy to discern. Coach and leader can sit outside the system, coming up with interventions that the leader then imposes upon the system. The leader seeks to control events.

2 First order – non-linear thinking
Coach and leader again see organisations as real systems, but many causal relationships are understood to be non-linear and circular. The leader recognises the need to avoid jumping to conclusions and spends more time analysing the system before making decisions.

3 Second order thinking
Through a second order lens, coach and leader see the system as complex and mysterious. They recognise the subjectivity of their own perceptions and take every opportunity to collaborate with others, sharing perspectives in a collective endeavour to come up with a joint hypothesis as to how the organisation-as-system might be operating.

4 Complexity thinking
Complexity theories tell us to focus on local interaction as well as wider patterns of behaviour. Interactions at a local level play out unpredictably, and interactions between different sub-systems result in what we see happening at a macro level. Coach and leader recognise that they are part of this activity. They cannot meaningfully think of themselves as neutral observers. They must seek to understand what is happening at the micro level and connect it to apparently random patterns of activity at the macro level.

5 Meta-systemic
This is the school of thought that says organisations are not systems at all. Organisations are not real and the boundaries we see between different systems and sub-systems are imaginary. Change emerges from interactions between people. People are self-aware, conscious and spontaneous, and the system metaphor isn't always

useful. This is the meta-systemic approach, and it says all talk of systems is metaphorical.

The boundaries between these five categories are not definitive. You may come across theories which seem to span categories. The categories are roughly chronological, in terms of the emergence of theories and frameworks, but there is no evidence to suggest that these are ways of thinking we pass through sequentially. The five categories are just a neat way of simplifying hundreds of theories about the ways systems work.

As you read through these accounts, of theory and practice, I urge you to resist the temptation to pigeonhole yourself as one or other of the five categories. I have spent much of the last two years sharing these ideas, at conferences and webinars. I often experience people trying to work out which of the five categories best describes their coaching. They usually choose one of the categories that seems most advanced. I doubt that this reflects reality. First order theories, with their emphasis on individual leadership and control, dominate the organisational narrative, a narrative in which we participate and co-create. Most of us encourage our coachees to make sense of the world by simplifying what they are experiencing and by identifying one or two points of leverage. We invite them to set goals and to commit to those goals. This is all first order practice, and most of us do it, sometimes. And there's nothing wrong with that. If I poke you in the eye, it hurts. Simple cause and effect. As Douglas Adams will later remind us, if it looks like a duck and quacks like a duck, it *probably* is a duck. Thinking first order is sometimes helpful, so I urge you not to exclude first order thinking too quickly from your self-identity as coach.

The best question here is not, 'Which way do I think?' The best question is, 'What access do I have to each of the ways of thinking?' If I have access only to first order ways of thinking, then I am fine so long as the duck is a duck. However, if the duck isn't actually a duck, and I keep assuming it is a duck, I am unlikely to be helpful. If I have access to other ways of thinking, then I experience myself stuck in the duck thing and consider other possibilities. Figure I.2 presents the five dimensions of systems thinking as layers. The more ways of thinking I have access to, the more likely I am to be useful. But sometimes the first order lens is all I need.

Figure I.2 represents five categories of systems thinking that have emerged roughly in this order. Management theories based on first order linear thinking emerged in the 1930s and 1940s. Milner's living systems theory was published in the 1970s and Senge's version of systems dynamics in the 1990s, the same decade that Gell-Man[10] and others published articles on complex adaptive systems. Ralph Stacey published the book *Complex Responsive Processes in Organisations* in 2001. This chronology is simplistic, since we can see the influence of much earlier work in all of the philosophies. Nor is it the case that each category builds neatly on the other. Some philosophies incorporate different categories of thinking. But I think the framework roughly represents an evolution of thinking. Nevertheless, as you read this book, remember I have greatly simplified a body of work that is deep, broad, far ranging and complicated. Don't feel obliged to work within the parameters of the framework I am sharing with you. Instead, I invite you to focus on coming up with your own definition of systemic. Consider which theories resonate best for you. Build your *own* model, a model that works best for you and that best reflects your practice and the coach you seek to be in the future.

You and your coach-self

How well do you currently know your coach self? How self-aware are you in terms of understanding which models and theories most inform your practice – and why? How well do you understand your purpose for coaching – what excites you when you get up in the morning? To what extent are you aware *how* you coach, and how that differs from what other coaches do? As we proceed through the book, I will share theories with you. I will offer ideas as to how different theoretical approaches are likely to show up in practice. I invite you to seize upon what is interesting and to integrate it into your coach-self. To make that easier, you will be invited in Chapter 1 to define your coach-self as it currently stands, before you begin reading. In other words, we will check on the foundations before trying to reconstruct the house. We will use a simple framework to do this, a model called the 3Ps – Philosophy, Purpose and Practice.[11]

To work through the 3Ps requires thinking through a series of questions. Suggested questions are presented in Chapter 1. You are encouraged to spend some time on working through the 3Ps in Chapter 1 before dashing into the chapters following. If that feels like a technical, tickbox, arm's-length exercise, then I'd invite you to consider it differently. You didn't become who you are as a coach arbitrarily. You are who you are as a coach because you are who you are as a person. Some models and approaches resonate with you more than others. Do you know why? Do you understand how what matters to you as a person is reflected in your coaching? At least two universities underpin their teachings by requiring students to consider their practice through the 3P lens, so you will be in good company.

Book structure

For each of the five categories, we will spend time understanding the essence of a few selected theories, before contrasting and comparing the categories through a consideration of the following five questions. What does each category have to say about each of the following?

- Systems
- The role of people in systems
- Change
- Power
- Team coaching

I have included team coaching in the list of questions because it seems to me that much of the current talk around team coaching is back to front. I have attended several courses/workshops on team coaching where the emphasis is on practice – what to do. I don't know how you can move to what you are *doing* as a team coach without spending time first considering how you are *thinking* as a team coach. Including how you think about systems.

For each of the five categories we will then consider how these theories translate into practice. What does coaching through each of these lenses look like and feel like? Kelly and Allen will help us translate theory into practice. Allen is the Marketing Director for Shoozon, and Kelly is his coach. We will visit Kelly and Allen at the end of each chapter as Kelly experiments with looking at the world through each of the five lenses. Building on Kelly's work with Allen, we will end each chapter with suggested characteristics of coaching through that particular lens. By the end of each chapter you may feel brain-fried, and so I direct you toward a movie, one that may help you integrate some of the material in a more relaxed environment.[12]

I hope you will read on, enjoy the book and come out the other end with a refined perspective as to who you are as a systemic coach. I would discourage you from asking yourself – am I systemic? We can answer that question right now. You *are* systemic. You are capable of standing back and seeing beyond your immediate relationship with your client. The vast majority of coaches are systemic in that they consider at least some aspects of what is happening in the coach's world. I would discourage you from categorising yourself. Likely you think and coach differently in different contexts. Instead, I invite you to consider your own definition of systemic. I invite you to define your own individual and personal approach to systemic coaching, a lens through which you can listen, filter and enquire whenever you hear someone talk about 'systemic coaching'.

Notes

1 Extract from Tony Abbott's 2017 speech to the Global Warming Policy Foundation (GWPF), www.theguardian.com/australia-news/2017/oct/10/tony-abbott-says-climate-change-is-probably-doing-good

2 Victor Kobayashi provides an interesting account of Bateson's work in Kobayashi, V.N. (1988). The Self-Reflexive Mind: The Life's Work of Gregory Bateson. *International Journal of Qualitative Studies in Education*, 1(4), 347–359.

3 Wolfgang Hofkirchner and David Rousseau in the foreword to the 2015 George Braziller published version of *General System Theory* by Ludwig von Bertalanffy.

4 Another oldish article, which just illustrates the challenge some of these ideas are taking to percolate: Lane, D.C., & Jackson, M.C. (1995). Only Connect! An Annotated Bibliography Reflecting the Breadth and Diversity of Systems Thinking. *Systems Research*, *12*(3), 217–228.

5 The Seven-Eyed Model is cited in lots of texts, including *Coaching, Mentoring and Organizational Consultancy* by Peter Hawkins and Nick Smith.

6 A quote by Peter Hawkins on page 169 of *Coaching and Mentoring Supervision Theory and Practice*, edited by Tatiana Bachkirova, Peter Jackson and David Clutterbuck.

7 The article by Tatiana Bachkirova and Carmelina Lawton Smith is a great read here: Bachkirova, T., & Lawton Smith, C. (2015). From Competencies to Capabilities in the Assessment and Accreditation of Coaches. *International Journal of Evidence Based Coaching and Mentoring*, *13*(2), 123–140.

8 Cambridge Dictionary.

9 von Bertalanffy, L. (2015). *General System Theory*. George Braziller.

10 Gell-Man, M. (1994). *The Quark and the Jaguar*. Freeman Press.

11 *The 3 Ps of Supervision and Coaching: Philosophy, Purpose and Process*, by Peter Jackson and Tatiana Bachkirova. Chapter 1 in the book *The Heart of Coaching Supervision* by Eve Turner and Stephen Palmer. I have changed 'Process' to 'Practice' in this book because practice seems most appropriate in this context.

12 Inspired by the 2017 article *Managing Chaos: Lessons from Movies on Chaos Theory* by Harri Raisio and Niklas Lundström, published in *Administration and Society*, *49*(2), 296–315.

1

You as coach

Some coaches have a prescribed methodology and approach that they have used for years, and that they have no intention of changing. Other coaches describe their practice as eclectic. If you ask them which models and frameworks they prefer, they will say – all of them. Some of these coaches understand lots of frameworks, but not necessarily in depth. Then there are the coaches who are continually exploring their craft, always eager to learn something new and work out how to put it into practice. For these coaches, being eclectic means something specific. These coaches have explored several approaches in depth. They can tell you which approaches really resonate with them and why.

If you believe that coaches need to access new ways of thinking in order to be most useful to the people we support, then you are likely excited at the prospect of exploring different approaches to systems thinking. You are used to challenging the way you think. To challenge the way that you think begins with an understanding of how you think now. So, in this chapter, I invite you to create some foundations upon which to build your exploration of what it means to be systemic. I will borrow an existing framework for this journey – the 3Ps framework detailed by Peter Jackson and Tatiana Bachkirova.[1] Peter and Tatiana write about the 3Ps in the context of coaching supervision, but the model applies equally well to coaching. In this chapter, I invite you to define your 3Ps. Creating the model is the beginning of our journey. The process of constructing the model should generate multiple insights as to how you currently coach and to your future development. Developing your 3Ps is not intended as a one-off exercise. I would encourage you to revisit it on a regular basis in service of nurturing your development.

In this book, the 3Ps stand for Philosophy, Purpose and Practice, and we will work through each P in building here a simple 3P model. You may want to use the worksheet in the Appendix to work through the rest of this chapter.

Philosophy

By philosophy we mean the ideas and theories that underpin your practice. Different coaches like different theories and have different experiences and beliefs. For example, Ann really likes theories of adult development because they have helped her build better relationships with her kids. George doesn't like theories of adult development because someone once assessed him, and it felt like they were putting him in a box. He isn't about to inflict the same misery on his clients. To understand our personal philosophy of coaching, we need to ask ourselves a series of questions.

What theories, models and frameworks especially appeal to you?

In answering this question, you are being asked to list the theories, models and frameworks that have made such an impression on you that they form the basis of your thinking much of the time. You are not being asked to write down every theory or model you have ever been exposed to. If the list is still long, pick the two, three or four that you hold most dear. You don't need to limit yourself to coaching-specific theories; there may be more general leadership theories, or theories from other disciplines that form a foundation for your practice.

Susan reflects on her coaching and identifies three theories/ models that particularly resonate for her. She lists:

1 Solutions-focussed approaches
2 Cognitive-behavioural models
3 Models of listening

That was the easy bit. Now ask yourself:

Why do these particular theories, models and frameworks appeal to you?

Do you know why the particular models and theories appeal to you? Even if you are a new coach, just finished your training, you were probably introduced to at least half a dozen approaches in your training. Which did you like best? And why?

Susan goes through her list one evening, exploring the question with a colleague. By the end of the evening she decides:

She likes solution-focussed approaches because they reflect her approach to life. She believes in thinking ahead, working out what to do next and not mulling too deeply on the past. She was like that as a child, she thinks, inspired by her mother, who was always there with a hug and an encouraging word as to her capacity to get things done. Her clients like the solution-focus too. Some talk critically about their experiences working with other coaches with whom it felt like being on a psychiatrist's couch. Susan believes in being boundaried, pragmatic and optimistic.

Susan likes cognitive-behavioural models. The idea that thoughts drive emotions drive behaviours is nice and simple. The framework enables her to help her coachees manage their emotions without delving too deeply into where those emotions may be coming from. Most clients find the idea of 'challenging the thought' a useful one and report immediate improvements in their ability to manage anxiety, frustration and anger. Susan reflects on her upbringing. Her parents didn't display much emotion and didn't encourage it in their children. She thinks her father's upbringing may have been quite traumatic, but no one talks about it. Susan believes people should talk about their feelings, in the right context, and finds cognitive-behavioural tools a useful way into the right level of conversation.

Susan thinks listening is important. For her there is more to listening than listening 'harder' or listening more 'actively'. She recognises within herself a tendency to move quickly to action, sometimes at the expense of asking questions to make sure she has really understood her clients' context. She reflects on her childhood and how hard it felt as a child to get her parents' attention. And she reflects on her corporate career and recognises how only a few leaders she worked with had this almost magical capacity to understand where she was coming from. They gave her their complete attention and refused to be distracted. She is determined to build the same presence into her coaching.

In answering these questions, Susan is bumping up against some fundamental aspects of self. For example, a propensity for action and getting things done. A desire to work with emotion, albeit without immersing herself too deeply into her emotions or others' emotions. A desire to be respectful and respected, and a belief that people need to sometimes slow down and notice each other when interacting.

Purpose

Our philosophy in life drives our purpose. Becoming more aware of the philosophies underlying our practice can help us become more purposeful. Many of us can be a little vague as to the reasons we coach. Some people say things like 'making a difference' without thinking more deeply about the nature of that difference.

Susan reflects on the answers she came up with under Philosophy. She evidently sees herself as someone high-energy and positive in outlook. When working in corporate, she found herself constantly encouraging those around her to better manage the barrage of demands being made upon their time. The general busy-ness of the business world squashes some people. Her purpose as a coach, she realises, is to help people keep their head above water, to stay happy and productive. People who keep moving forward don't sink. She helps people work through issues quickly, to prioritise and to focus their energies on making things happen. The more individuals she touches in an organisation, the more effective and efficient that organisation is likely to be.

Some people prefer to start with Purpose instead of Philosophy. The logic is that the theories, tools and frameworks you like are determined by your purpose as a coach.

Practice

Our Philosophy and Purpose underpin how we Practice. If I like solutions-focussed approaches and am driven to move people forward, then you may see me encouraging my coaches to come up with goals quickly, for example. In asking you about your Practice, quite simply, we are asking – what would the proverbial fly on the wall see if it followed you through a coaching assignment? How do you set up a coaching assignment? What actually happens in the coaching room? This would include your approach to taking a briefing, your strategy for engaging other stakeholders in the organisation, how you agree with a client whether the assignment has been successful or not, how you open a session, any tools and models you make use of, how you end an assignment, etc.

Susan likes the GROW model, even though she hears it criticised as being overly simplistic. Starting the conversation by talking about goals is consistent with her solutions-focussed approach. Of course, she doesn't always start by talking goals – not if the client is determined to talk about the current reality first. Nor does she use the model in a rigidly linear way, and she is quite flexible as to the level of the goal. Sometimes goals can be very specific, other times they can be broad and more a description of an overarching purpose. But she will always encourage her clients to stay focussed on outcomes and finds that the GROW model helps her in that regard.

In taking an initial briefing from an organisation, she is used to clients spending a lot of time talking about a potential coachee's shortcomings and what needs to be fixed. When this happens, she always tries to shift the client into thinking about a solution, about what success would look like. She asks them what role they might play in helping the coachee to be successful.

Susan makes full use of a customised version of a cognitive-behavioural approach. She has her own spreadsheet which invites coachees to consider how thoughts lead to emotions lead to behaviours when triggered by a particular issue. On the second half of the spreadsheet, the coachee is encouraged to challenge the thought and to come up with a few specific experiments to think and act differently.

Susan makes sure her coachees always come up with actions at the end of every session. She sends them an email a week before every session to remind them to complete their actions, and she starts every session by asking the coachee what they did to complete their actions.

Once you have completed your 3Ps, the next question to ask yourself is, does it all hang together? Susan's model appears to be coherent. If, on the other hand, she had cited narrative coaching in her Philosophy, with an emphasis on exploring the past and letting intentions emerge, then the Practice she described might have looked odd.

The 3Ps and being systemic

John, Anne and Sean are three coaches. John calls himself a systemic coach. Working with coachees, he always makes a point of asking himself 'who else is involved here?' When coachees talk about feeling anxious or worried, he always explores what or who is triggering that anxiety, rather than assume the coachee is naturally anxious. An example is the case of Mark, who finally worked out that his anxiety was triggered by his boss, who reminded him of an old colleague, who reminded him of his mother, who always smacked his hand when he was slow to explain his misdemeanours. As a consequence of their discussion, Mark made special efforts to manage his emotions when in the presence of his line manager and always tried to see her point of view, even when she was criticising him. To John, being systemic includes exploring someone's upbringing and the impact of other people from the past.

Anne also calls herself a systemic coach, but upon listening to John's story in group supervision, she doesn't think her approach and John's approach have much in common. When John told the story of Mark, Anne found herself wondering about the culture of the organisation, the history of that culture and how that culture was being perpetuated. The prevailing culture, it seemed to Anne, was having an impact not just on Mark, but on everyone else in the story as well. If she was John, she would encourage Mark to understand more deeply the dynamics of that culture and work out ways to disrupt it. Understanding your family of origin may be useful sometimes, but to be systemic also means looking at other factors in the system *now*, and how those factors are impacting the scenario being described by the coachee.

Sean also thinks of himself as a systemic coach. John's perspective, it seems to him, whilst systemic in the sense that it acknowledges the impact of family systems, is overly individualistic. Anne is thinking more holistically, but she seems overly inclined to assume that A + B leads to C. For example, she said that Mark should talk to the CEO about starting a piece of work on culture change. Her description of a culture change programme sounded quite linear and top down to him, unlikely to have the desired impact. Anne's version of systemic would be better if she started thinking more about power dynamics.

John, Anne and Sean are all systemic coaches, but their versions of systemic are all different. We could simply choose which version we like best, but in this book, we invite you to define your personal version of systemic, exploring the wisdom of all three approaches.

Your mission (should you choose to accept it)

You may be asking yourself – why should I spend time on this exercise? I coach intuitively and I am eclectic – I draw on all sorts of models and theories. Why do I need to write it all down? My answer would be to challenge yourself. Really, how self-aware is your coaching self? To what extent do you understand the lens through which you relate to your clients? To what extent do you know why you say the things that you say, and why you stay quiet when you stay quiet? To what extent do you understand the role you play in shaping your client's intentions?

You may not feel inclined to write an essay on the 3Ps. In that case, just write a few notes under each heading, whatever it takes to begin articulating – who are you as a coach? Clarity helps you to identify blind spots, ways of thinking and coaching that have escaped your attention. Clarity helps you understand the extent to which you have fully leveraged those philosophies you already subscribe to. And clarity will help you make sense of these different ways of thinking about systems.

In the last few years I have come across many coaches who say they identify with complexity theories, for example. But watching them coach in class and in workshops and listening to them talk about how they coach in supervision, I find myself questioning the extent to which these theories have been fully integrated into their Practice. The Philosophy appears half-chewed and semi-digested. Most coaches I know align themselves with complexity theories, but watching them coach, I more often see signs of simple, linear, cause and effect. I see it in my own coaching too. There is a difference between what we say we do and what we actually do. Reflecting on the 3Ps helps us to become more self-aware and more impactful.

Susan's 3Ps model will appeal to some of you and not to others. All coaches are different. But there are aspects of Susan's model that don't sit well when viewed through some of the five lenses. Susan gets great feedback from her clients, but that does not mean she is having the impact she thinks she is. What appears to be brilliant coaching from a first order lens may be quite damaging when viewed through a second order lens. This ultimately is for Susan to decide. The question is, how much time is she prepared to invest in exploring different Philosophies, and the extent to which that thinking feeds through to Purpose and Practice?

Your mission here, should you choose to accept it, is to think through the 3Ps and to write at least a few notes for each. I then invite you, as you work through this book, to note down which systems theories get you thinking, what practices appeal to you. Does your purpose for coaching evolve? Be innovative. Be creative. Talk it through with colleagues. Feel empowered.

The book is structured to make this easy as possible. Each chapter covers one way of thinking about systems; a Philosophy. Each chapter then asks you to review your Purpose in the light of that theory, and then think about Practice. At the end of the book I will invite you to review your 3Ps and conclude how they have changed over the course of your reading.

Note

1 The 3 Ps of supervision and coaching: Philosophy, Purpose and Process, by Peter Jackson and Tatiana Bachkirova, Chapter 2 in *The Heart of Coaching Supervision* by Eve Turner and Stephen Palmer.

2

First order linear thinking

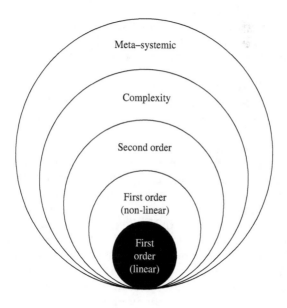

Theory in a nutshell

Frederick Winslow Taylor and scientific management

Frederick Winslow Taylor was an engineer. He watched people engage in manual work and noticed how inefficient they were. He watched people shovelling coal, for example, and saw that they used the same shovels to lift rice coal at 3½ pounds per shovel as they did to lift a much heavier coal at 38 pounds per shovel. Through observation he worked out that the optimum load per shovel was 22 pounds, and he arranged for a range of shovels to be made available for use with different types of coal. As a consequence, Bethlehem Steel were able to slim their workforce by 75% and increase profitability by 60%.

Taylor summed up his approach in five simple principles:[1]

1 Shift responsibility for the organisation of work from the worker to the manager
2 Use scientific methods to determine the most efficient way of doing the work
3 Select the best person to perform the newly designed job
4 Train the worker to do the work efficiently
5 Monitor performance to ensure procedures are followed and results obtained

This is organisation-as-machine, and people are the cogs. The manager is the objective observer, the system designer, deciding the rules by which the machine functions. The idea of organisation-as-machine may sound quaintly old-fashioned, but these ideas still prevail. Writing job descriptions, for example, is consistent with the idea we can standardize jobs. Job descriptions make sense if a job can be precisely defined and the environment remains unchanged. They remove the need for people to make choices about what they do. There are many examples of the organisation-as-machine approach being useful, facilitating productivity transformation and rapid growth. If we look at McDonald's through this lens, for example, we see people in our local restaurant doing the exact same things people in other restaurants do. Staff can be trained quickly and cheaply to perform the same simple tasks their counterparts are performing all over the world. This approach has served McDonald's well in terms of business growth. It works well when the operation can be broken down into simple, straightforward tasks and when the environment doesn't change.

Elton Mayo and theories of motivation

Being the cog in a machine isn't very exciting. Jobs are designed to be repetitive, with the emphasis on repeating the same sequence of activities with increasing efficiency. People get tired and bored. Elton Mayo, at the Hawthorne Plant of the Western Electric Company in Chicago, studied motivation in the workplace. He found that workers performed at their best only when they were motivated. Organisational psychologists showed how motivation depends on autonomy, responsibility and recognition.[2] The discipline of human resource management emerged, as did the framing of people as a special kind of resource that needs to be managed differently. This approach neatly splits the leader's role into managing task and managing people. We still see this binary scoping of the leader's role everywhere we go, in definitions of leadership and the dominant narrative around the individual leader's ability to 'get the job done' and 'bring people on the journey'.

Norbert Wiener and cybernetics

Norbert Wiener was a professor of mathematics at the Massachusetts Institute of Technology (MIT). During the Second World War, British scientists were called upon to improve the design of anti-aircraft systems. Too many German planes were breaking through the Allies' defences and dropping bombs on England. Wiener, an American, invented the Wiener Filter, a mathematical approach to predicting the future movements of enemy planes based on past movements and ongoing feedback. The Wiener Filter filtered out all extraneous noise, leaving only core data visible. He and his colleagues modelled the movements of particular bombers, including unmanned V1s. The mathematical models worked so well that American guns fitted with Wiener Filters achieved a 99% success rate in shooting down planes as they entered Britain.

Building on this work after the war, Wiener pioneered the development of cybernetics. The basic premise of cybernetics is really quite simple. If I bowl a bowling ball on a bowling green and the bowl runs too long, then next time I bowl the ball, I apply less force. If the next bowl runs too short, then I apply more force, and so on, until I get the weight just right. I am changing the amount of force I am applying based on visual and proprioceptive feedback. Wiener believed that feedback loops are important in all intelligent behaviour, that we are continually comparing actual performance with desired performance and making decisions based on feedback on past efforts.

This may remind you of goal theory. Consider Figure 2.1, a diagram from a paper on goals by Anthony Grant (eminent

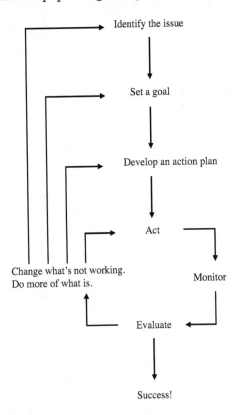

Figure 2.1 A generic model of goal-directed self-regulation
Source: Grant (2012)

coaching psychologist).[3] Imagine coach and coachee talk-ing about the coachee's desire to have greater influence on stakeholders (*identify the issue*). The coachee *sets a goal*; that she will develop the ability to deliver high-impact presenta-tions. She *develops an action plan*, which includes making a presentation the next week. She commits to prepare for the presentation and to practise it until she can deliver it without notes. Then she delivers the presentation (*act*). She makes a point of asking feedback from those she trusts in the audience (*monitor*). They tell her that her presentation was much improved, that she spoke clearly and that they understood most of what she said. They also suggest she make more eye contact; she spent much of the presentation looking at a spot on the ceiling. As a result, she missed sev-eral cues, instances where people frowned or looked at each other, uncertain what she was trying to say. With the help of her coach, she *evaluates* her efforts and concludes that the presentation was in many respects successful. She needs to keep preparing and practising. However, she commits to do relaxation exercises before the next presentation so she is not daunted at engaging more intimately with her audience. She modifies her action plan and prepares to act again.

Notice the bowling ball effect. The coachee has a goal in mind, which is to deliver a great presentation. She comes up with a plan to achieve her goal and implements it. The ball gets close to the jack in that she does a good presenta-tion, but still stops a little way short. So, the coachee makes some changes to the bowling of her next ball, hoping her next presentation is even better. Notice also the linearity of cause and effect. Just as we are assuming that the only factor influencing the travelling of the bowling ball is the amount of force applied by the bowler, so we are assuming that preparation, practice and relaxation are the three fac-tors that directly determine whether or not an audience enjoys a presentation.

These are three slants on the idea of organisation as machine. People are the cogs in the machine. The leader needs to ensure the system is designed with the cogs in the right places doing the right things. The leader needs to motivate the cogs and the leader needs access to feedback, to monitor how well the machine is running. The scientific management perspective encourages us to stand outside the 'machine' to diagnose its functioning and amend its design. The motivational perspective reminds us to pay special attention to the human components of the machine, making sure they stay happy and engaged. The cybernetics model explicitly acknowledges the open boundary between the inside of the machine and the environment in which it is operating. Feedback mechanisms ensure the machine responds appropriately to changes happening outside its boundaries. This is how many people view the functioning of an organisation. Leadership programmes focus on task and relationship and multi-rater 360 surveys proliferate, providing individual leaders with feedback as to their capacity to get things done and motivate people.

Philosophy

A coach thinking through a first order linear lens is likely to adopt the following perspectives:

1 Perspective on system
Through this lens we see the organisation as a machine. Connections between the machine parts are straightforward and easy to understand. The scientific manager's quest is to design the system to deliver best outcomes, like the Formula 1 Head Engineer charged with delivering next season's racing engine. The organisation, like the car engine, has real boundaries dividing the inside of the engine from the surrounding environment. Unlike a car engine, the component parts of this machine are people. People require special attention, but they are still components, performing their roles as defined by job descriptions. These components need to be motivated, however. Motivation is the fuel that drives the engine. Cybernetics reminds us that you cannot design an engine without building in feedback mechanisms. If the air temperature gets too hot, then the engine needs cooling down. If the engine rattles, we need to tighten a screw. If the individ-

ual is working too slowly, we need to incentivise them to work faster.

2 Perspective on people

People perform two roles in the first order system. Most people are expected to be passive and compliant. They must do as they are supposed to if the system is going to function as designed. This is the first part of Frederick Winslow Taylor's first principle of scientific management; that the worker has no say in organising the work. On the other hand, *some* people in the system, the leaders, get to stand outside the system and tweak its design. This is consistent with the second part of Taylor's first principle; that managers design work. The manager therefore has two roles. First, when standing outside the system it is her role to design the system. Second, once the system has been designed, she joins everyone else back in the system performing her role as designed.

The coach is not part of the system. The coach visits the manager's office when the manager is in outside-system mode to help her decide what needs to be done to the system. The coach sees himself as neutral, an occasional visitor, but not part of the system. Coach and coachee believe that the leader can step outside the melee of the day, make a plan, then return back into the melee and implement that plan, redirecting the organisation to go where she wants it to go. The coach helps her to review how to exert her control as a leader. The idea that the leader cannot control events within her organisation is anathema. Some organisations make it clear that they expect the coach to deliver specific outcomes, and some coaches accept that challenge, believing they will be successful if the leader is persuaded to exert their power appropriately

3 Perspective on change

The organisation-as-machine does not change itself. Change does not come from within. The system designer designs the organisation/machine and monitors its performance to make sure it does what it is supposed to do. If performance deviates from expectations, because people make mistakes, or perform too slowly, etc., then the problem must be fixed, and thus equilibrium is restored. Maintaining equilibrium is an objective and discordance is seen as a threat to stability and efficiency. Conflict within the organisation is seen as a bad thing. Conflict suggests that something isn't working properly and needs to be fixed. Good change is something that can come only from the designer of the system, from outside. This might be the senior leadership of the organisation, or the head of a division, or the leader of a team. The emphasis is on control and stability. If the organisation is looking at the world through this lens, then it seeks certainty. That means it will likely seek commitments from its coaches that specific outcomes will be delivered within defined time periods. When coach and leader sit down together, the leader is the system designer, deciding what she needs to do to improve the functioning of the organisation, or part of the organisation. Change is something that is done to a system, or an organisation. It must be carefully planned. It has a beginning, a middle and an end. The leader feels responsible for change and the only change that happens otherwise is a consequence of entropy – slow deterioration.

4 Perspective on power

Power is centralised in the system designer. Everyone else in the system is expected to perform as decided by the system designer. Positional power is sacrosanct and resides in the leader. Leadership is about the capacity of the individual leader to operate independently and autonomously. This mantra still pervades 90% of leadership and coaching literature. Even though derided in some texts as the 'great man' theory of leadership, this emphasis on the characteristics of the individual pervades. The individual leader is seen as the brains behind the operation, the instigator of change and the guardian of culture. Leadership, through this lens, may be a team sport, but the team has a readily identifiable leader who is wholly responsible for outcomes. The individual leader is generously rewarded when things go well, and often dismissed when things go wrong. If a football team loses six games in a row, then the Board sacks the manager. It is up to the new manager to then work out what else may need to happen if the team is to start winning. The same applies in corporate and politics. If the organisation isn't performing well, then people look to the CEO. Are they up to the job? If the economy isn't going well, then attention turns to the performance of the Prime Minister. The inference is clear – that the leader of an organisation has control. The coach operating through this lens holds the leader accountable for the outcome of his actions. She assumes that the leader's sphere of influence is wide. The coach encourages the coachee to similarly hold his staff to account for their deliverables and to take action should the desired results not be forthcoming.

5 Perspective on team coaching

An effective team defined through this lens is a group of people with clearly defined roles. The focus of team coaching is on ensuring that each person on the team understands their role in the machine and manages their part of the machine efficiently. Processes are well defined, and everyone in every function also understands their role and responsibilities. The link between processes in one function and processes in another function are clearly understood. If changes are made in one part of the organisation, then the implications for other parts of the organisation are identified and actioned. The leader of the team is the head-designer and has final say on all decisions.

Purpose

A coach thinking this way values the relationship with her coachee and spends most of her time with him. Her purpose is likely to be around helping the coachee to have an immediate impact on the organisation through exercising his individual 'greatness'. She may talk about the importance of individual accountability and her role in helping individuals develop greater integrity. She is a likely advocate of the mantra 'changing an organisation one person at a time'. She believes in hierarchy, and if her stated purpose is about helping the organisation as well as the individual, then it will be about helping the organisation to develop great leaders.

Practice

Kelly and Allen

Let's now touch base with Kelly and Allen for the first time. Kelly is coaching Allen. Allen is the Marketing and Sales Director for Shoozon, a company that manufactures and distributes shoes for children. Allen has been in the role for six months and is struggling. He is spending more and more hours in the office, but his efforts are having minimal impact on performance. Sales had been on a trajectory of steady growth for six years prior to his taking the role. Now sales are stagnant, even in slight decline. He is spending time with the marketing team, urging them to come up with a big new campaign, and time with the sales staff trying to find out why consumers are spending less in-store. The CEO wants to know when sales will start climbing again and the HR Director is concerned that Allen's staff think they are being micro-managed.

Part 1

Kelly and Allen have a conversation. Allen spends the first 30 minutes explaining what is going on and telling Kelly how stressed he is feeling.

Kelly: Sales are declining, you are working really hard and your staff are feeling micro-managed?

Allen: Yes.

Kelly: How are your competitors doing?

Allen: Industry sales are 3% up.

Kelly: What's happening across the product range?

Allen: Some markets are slowing down more than others, you're right. We have to make some choices.

Kelly: What's employee engagement like? Do you have any data?

Allen: The last pulse survey said it's sitting at 58%, down 10% from last year.

Kelly: And what's changed, do you think, to result in the fall-off in sales?

Allen: I think it's because we had a few key staff leave. The market intelligence guy was up for my role and resigned when he didn't get it. And we have some new people in sales who haven't yet hit the ground running.

Kelly: So, you need a good market intelligence person and you need to upskill your salespeople fast?

Allen: I think so.

Kelly: If you woke up tomorrow and the world was a wonderful place, what would you be seeing and hearing and feeling?

Allen: I'd have a great team in place. Sales would be back where they were. Staff would all know what they were doing and would be happy doing it. And I could leave them to it for a couple of weeks and go on holiday.

Kelly: So, what needs to happen?

Allen: Well, I need to do some recruitment obviously, now you've pointed it out. I need to get some mentoring happening. I need my managers to be happier and to feel more empowered. And I need to claw back some time somewhere.

Kelly: What will you do?

Allen: I'm going to kick off the recruitment process, get one of my experienced regional guys to spend six months bringing the newbies up to speed and I'm going to talk to Helen and Sean. They are both capable and they have both complained that I spend too much time overseeing their work. Time for them both to show me they can get things done without me looking over their shoulders.

Kelly: I look forward to seeing how it goes!

Part 2

A month later they meet again.

Kelly: What's been happening?

Allen: Look, things have improved. Sean's marketing team came up with a new social media campaign which involved no discounting, even though I would definitely have cut prices. I've bitten my tongue so often I'm surprised I can still talk to you.

Kelly: Good news!

Allen: Yes. And Helen's sales team is now working closely with Sean's marketing team, effectively leveraging our online marketing presence in-store. Sales are definitely up, and they wouldn't have gone up had I not delegated more.

Kelly: What else?

Allen: We have a couple of good candidates for the marketing intelligence role and the sales guys are definitely taking more accountability.

Kelly: Great! And what feedback have you received?

Allen: People are happier. A couple of times I slipped back into old habits, telling Sean what he should do. But he reminded me what I had said and actually told me to 'butt out'.

Kelly: How did you feel about that?

Allen: Great that he said it and didn't just think it.

Coaching through this lens

Based on a first order–linear philosophy, we might expect a coach to show some of the following traits. Remember that most of us behave this way at least some of the time.

1 Searching for simple causal relationships

The coach thinking through this lens envisages the organisation as a real system operating according to a set of simple linear rules. In the scenario just presented, Allen spent 30 minutes or more telling Kelly all of his frustrations and interpretations of events. Kelly listened intently, filtering what Allen said and deciding what was meaningful, what was less relevant and what was missing. Kelly's thinking mirrors the functioning of a Wiener Filter; filtering out all the noise so that the anti-aircraft guns can correctly forecast the trajectory of incoming bombs. Kelly has her Wiener Filter firmly in place. Allen's story meanders. Her filter sifts through the noise and fluff of Allen's story to identify the root cause of the issue, some lovely simple cause and effect. She asked the question about market data because she felt it was missing from Allen's account. She asked him a lot of other questions in order to build a more detailed picture in her mind as to what was going on. As Allen talks, she becomes excited. The departure of the market intelligence guy, the new untrained sales staff and the way he is managing Sean and Helen, all intuitively feel significant. If he hires a new market intelligence guy, the team will understand better what's happening in the market. If Allen trains up his sales staff, in-store sales will go up. If he stops micro-managing Sean and Helen, they will be more motivated and effective. She is a coach, though, and so she doesn't tell Allen these issues represent the crux of his problem. She hypothesises, and Allen agrees with her hypothesis. It can be helpful to think of ourselves as coaches wearing our Wiener Filters over our eyes like a pair of goggles. These goggles are part of who we are; we can't take them off. Through our Wiener Filters we see what we are looking for and dismiss the rest as irrelevant. The limitation of this approach is obvious; we all wear different Wiener Filters. The judgements we make as to what is important is subjective. We will return to this point in Chapter 4.

2 Focus on goals and actions to achieve

Once Allen indicates he knows what the issue is, Kelly straightaway asks him what he will do. Allen comes up with specific actions, based on his hypothesis, and commits to making those actions happen. Kelly encourages Allen to engage with her in the goal-directed self-regulation process referred to earlier in this chapter. For Kelly, the hypothesis they came up with around cause and effect is sufficient to move into purposeful action. This is very much traditional coaching in action.

3 Respecting boundaries

Implicit to the way Kelly and Allen are both talking is the idea of organisation as a system, with clearly demarcated boundaries between functions. Allen talks about the sales team and the marketing team and at one point alludes to the relationship between the two teams. He doesn't mention anyone else in the organisation except for the CEO and HR Director, both of whom he needs to keep happy if he is to be successful. Allen is implicitly thinking about his organisation as a hierarchical system, and about his own marketing and sales teams as sub-systems within the bigger system. Kelly doesn't challenge his thinking. She doesn't ask about other characters inside or outside the organisation. Nor does she challenge the implicit idea that the marketing and sales team actually do operate as two distinct entities.

4 Change as a programme

Allen talks about events as a story with a before, a during and an after. Before he took up the new role, sales were good. Now sales are bad. This story will end when sales return to where they were before. He needs to find a strategy that will deliver that ending. That strategy will involve his tweaking the system, putting it right and restoring equilibrium. Coach and coachee often collude in talking about stability as the norm. The coach acts and speaks in line with this philosophy and talks about change and what is required to effect change successfully and to bed it down.

5 Focussing on the individual

The coach is often happy coaching individuals and sees little to be gained by bringing the coachee together with other people as part of the coaching. Collective gatherings are the domain of the coachee, attempting to put into practice individual commitments forged in the heat of the coaching room. Whether or not the coachee is successful depends on their individual commitment and ability. This is the old organisational development (OD) philosophy that says you can change the world one person at a time. This philosophy pays little attention to the impact that leaders have on each other. The coach supports organisational attempts to help individuals become better leaders. The more, the merrier. If every leader improves their individual performance, then it is inevitable that the organisation as a whole will do better. A collection of effective individuals is bound to bring the organisation success.

The coach may regard the individual through a 'right and wrong' lens. The individuals' capacity to be a good leader is framed in terms of generic competencies. There is therefore a right and wrong way to lead based on an adherence to a competency framework. The coach may sometimes be experienced as directive, for example when debriefing the outcome of multi-rater 360 surveys. The coach encourages the coachee to change his behaviour in response to others' ratings and may even tell him he is 'resistant to change' if he does not take on board the feedback.

Leading through this lens

This way of thinking about organisation-as-system is pervasive. The organisation is a system and is only as good as the quality of its parts. To improve the effectiveness of the organisation, we need to continually improve the quality of its components. Employees are expected to achieve specific outcomes within specific timeframes. The better they are at meeting those expectations, the more likely they are to be promoted, earn more money and enjoy greater status. The role of the leader is to ensure the performance of his part of the machine. Signs of this philosophy at play in the leader include:

- A focus on specific objectives, KPIs and a job description
- A strong belief in individual accountability
- Issuing instruction, and getting frustrated when those instructions are not carried out
- A dual mindset, that frames 'soft skills' (the motivation bit) with 'hard skills' (getting the job done)
- A grudging acceptance of the need for feedback – grudging because the purpose of feedback is to tell me where I am going wrong; where the machine needs fixing

- Expecting more senior leaders to sort out high-level issues, in line with their pay grade
- An evident dislike of 'office politics', which is a time-wasting consequence of senior leaders not making tough decisions

Not all of these characteristics necessarily imply first order linear thinking, of course. Reality is complex, and we should beware the temptation to assume certainty in our diagnosis of others' behaviours. But we can listen, and we can hypothesise and probe. Imagine a team that is not hitting its targets. A leader thinking though a first order lens is likely to focus only on individual performance. Who are hitting their targets, and who are not? The leader will talk to those who are not hitting their targets and urge them to do better, becoming frustrated if the individual wants to stop and talk about why those targets are unattainable. Or the leader may invest a lot of energy in incentivising performance, doing everything he can to keep staff happy and engaged. Again, he will expect to see performance improve as a consequence. If poor performance appears to be a consequence of leaders up the line not taking decisive action, for example, not taking steps to push performance in other functions, then this leader will get frustrated. The organisation is a machine, and every cog and every wheel needs to be doing its part.

Developing leaders

In many organisations we train our leaders to manage this way. Ralph Stacey describes leadership development programmes as 'institutionalized techniques of discipline'[4] In other words, leaders are trained by their organisations to organise people and make sure they do what they are supposed to do. The participant is told how they are expected to demonstrate leadership. Programmes are structured around lists of competencies approved by senior management, and participants are expected to learn these competencies and put them into action.

In some organisations we encounter the 'authenticity paradox'. This is where the leader is encouraged to be authentic and/or autonomous, while at the same time being pulled to comply with the expectations of the organisation. Leaders are being asked to set a personal vision for their team, which may sound like the leader has freedom to define a new future. In reality, senior leaders in the organisation have already established a direction. The leader is in fact being asked to come up with a message that motivates people to align to that pre-existing vision. Little wonder, then, that in introducing the notion of coaching to leaders, so often I hear leaders define coaching as the art of 'getting people to decide for themselves to do what I want them to do.' This may represent their own experience of being 'empowered.'

Stacey suggests that the real purpose of leadership programmes is to teach employees how to exercise disciplinary power more effectively. Leadership becomes the art of coercive persuasion. Such programmes don't change people in any fundamental way. They train them to persuade others to comply and conform. We see this narrative play itself out in the conversation around values, for example. Many organisations have a half-dozen or so core values. There is nothing wrong with organisations espousing common values, so long as we recognise them for what they are. These are not deeply held personal values shared by everyone in the organisation. They are rules of behaviour, established by the organisation, that everyone working for the organisation is expected to conform to. Your values are not the issue. What matters is how you behave.

Leadership programmes inevitably reflect the way that programme commissioners and designers think. Stacey points out that many of those commissioning programmes work in HR functions and have not had significant leadership experience of their own.[5] This is not always true, but it does serve to remind us that if organisations are to access new ways of thinking, then programme designers need to consider the limitations of their own thinking. Many programme designers think through a first order lens. The paradigm is that leaders who learn and apply new skills will be more effective leaders. We can design leadership programmes to teach people new skills and/or we can design leadership programmes to help people think differently. If we are interested in helping leaders think differently, then programme designers must question their own thinking first. If you ask the business what it wants, you will receive a response through its existing lens.

Why does any of this matter to you, the coach? First, many leadership programmes incorporate coaching. The espoused purpose of this coaching is often to help people put into practice the skills they have learned at workshops independent of the participant's perspective on those skills. If you see the world through Stacey's eyes, then you may experience yourself being asked to collude in coercive persuasion, covert institutionalisation. Do you oblige? Or do you find yourself challenging teaching materials, much to the annoyance of your client? Where do you stand on this? Second, many organisations either have realised or are beginning to realise that this approach to leadership development may not be serving them well. The idea that we can programme leaders to tackle complex issues through the language of generic competency frameworks is being increasingly challenged. What, then, do organisations replace traditional leadership development programmes with? Do you have a view? What is your role in helping organisations think through how to make these kinds of programmes more effective? Is that part of your purpose?

At the movies

In a fun paper, Harri Raisio and Niklas Lundstrom illustrate three different approaches to systems thinking through an account of three movies.[6] The first movie is *The Butterfly Effect*. The central character in the movie is Evan. As a young adult, Evan discovers that he can travel back in time and change his actions. Each time he returns to his past to change an action, he triggers a new future. These alternative futures include becoming a college student, a prison inmate and a double amputee. There are often dreadful consequences for Evan or one of his friends. Evan never succeeds in engineering the future he is looking for. In the director's cut of the movie, Evan becomes despondent and engineers a way to kill himself.

If we watch the movie through our systems thinking lens, then we can see Evan the linear realist. He believes in his capacity to instigate actions that will lead, through simple linear causal relationships, to predictable desired outcomes. Evan believes that life follows simple rules, that A + B leads to C. He just needs to work out what the rules are so he can manipulate the system. Evan believes he can stand outside of his life, plot an intervention, change outcomes and return to a newly designed life. He wants to be both the architect of his life and a participant in his life. As a consequence of those beliefs, Evan keeps coming with plans, he keeps monitoring outcomes and he keeps tweaking his plans and trying again. But Evan's plans never result in his achieving his goals. In the end he gives up, disheartened to the point of despair, ultimately thwarted in his desire to control his world.

There are parallels here to what happens in many organisations. For example, there is the bank that wanted all their frontline staff to engage in on-selling. They ran a pilot and proved (to themselves) that on-selling leads to increased sales. They changed reward and recognition strategies to encourage staff to on-sell. They changed computer systems and sent 'coaches' out to the branches to teach staff how to use the new system. All were very logical actions designed to shift the behaviour of staff. But their strategies failed, no matter how many new initiatives they came up with. Staff had been recruited for their capacity to empathise with customers. They saw that their customers didn't like being sold to, and so they didn't do it. Senior leaders were called to account by other senior leaders, rebuked because they didn't achieve promised outcomes. Failure was attributed to the failure of individuals, and new senior leaders were recruited. The core failure, however, was to fail to recognise the limitations of first order linear systems thinking.

Your 3Ps

I hope when you read the story of Kelly and Allen, you found yourself wondering, 'What's wrong with the way Kelly is coaching here?' I hope you have some idea what I meant when I said, don't dismiss the possibility that you operate through this first order lens sometimes. I think most coaches do. I don't personally see that as a problem, so long as we know we are doing it and have access to other approaches too. Now may be a good time to stop, reflect and ask yourself some questions. What sense do you make of this way of thinking about systems?

1 At the beginning of this chapter we looked at Winslow's theory of scientific management, Mayo's theories on motivation and cybernetics. What was useful about each of the three theories? They each have their limitations, but what was *useful*?
2 If you review your Purpose again now, has it changed at all? Can it be further refined?
3 What insights have you gained as to how you coach now – what is your Practice?
4 Do you coach differently in different contexts? If so, what triggers you in each context?
5 Do you have a glimpse yet of what other practical approaches you might seek to integrate in your practice?

Segue . . .

Kelly and Allen meet again six weeks later.

Kelly: You look distressed.

Allen: I am. Things went fine for a while, but then sales suddenly dropped 20%. No one knows why. The market is flat, but it hasn't fallen 20%. The CEO is back at my door making vague threatening remarks. It's terrible.

Kelly: How has the team responded?

Allen: They're miserable as anyone. I've had to step in again. I can't sit on the sidelines while no one has a plan for putting things right.

Kelly: Helen and Sean?

Allen: Sean told me to butt out again, but I got cross. We're not playing games here. We have to fix sales and fix them quickly. Either something's going on and no one is telling me, or no one knows what they're doing. Either way, I have to roll my sleeves up until we find a way out of this mess.

Kelly: No more delegation?

Allen: Sorry, Kelly. I have got to manage us out of this one myself.

Kelly asks Allen lots more questions, all of which Allen answers, concisely and clearly. He is a man with a plan, and the plan is to work all the hours he needs to in order to resolve the crisis. He postpones the next two sessions. 'What next?' she wonders.

Notes

1   Taylor, F.W. (1911). *Principles of Scientific Management*. Harper & Row. Summarised in Morgan, G. (2006). *Images of Organization*. Sage.

2   Mayo, E. (1933). *The Human Problems of an Industrial Civilisation*. Macmillan. Summarised in Morgan, G. (2006). *Images of Organization*. Sage.

3   Grant, A.M. (2012). An Integrated Model of Goal-Focused Coaching: An Evidence-Based Framework for Teaching and Practice. *International Coaching Psychology Review*, 7(2), 146–165.

4   Stacey, R. (2012). *Tools and Techniques of Leadership and Management*. Routledge.

5   Stacey, R. (2012). *Tools and Techniques of Leadership and Management*. Routledge.

6   Raisio, H. & Lundstrom, N. (2017). Managing Chaos: Lessons from Movies on Chaos Theory. *Administration and Society*, 49(2), 296–315.

3

First order non-linear thinking

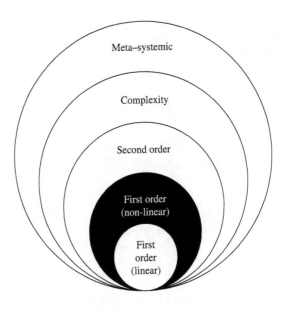

Theory in a nutshell

Peter Senge and systems dynamics

Peter Senge and colleagues identified five disciplines required by a learning organisation, one of which was systems thinking. Systems thinking, as defined by Senge, is about looking beyond simple linear cause and effect. To understand how a system works, you also need to look for positive reinforcing feedback and causal loops. Cybernetics looks at negative feedback. For example, the boiler heats up the water, the water temperature gets too high and the system sends a message to the boiler to switch itself off. Positive feedback would be a system in which as the water heats up, the system keeps telling the boiler to keep boiling. This wouldn't be very useful, and the boiler would explode. But these positive reinforcing loops do exist. If I give my partner a bunch of flowers and she gives me a big kiss, then I might go out and buy more flowers. If I like being kissed, then very quickly my house will fill with flowers, and keep on filling with flowers. Sometimes such patterns are hard to discern because there is a time lag between cause and effect. For example, my partner gives me a kiss. Then I go to work and she calls me to complain that I didn't feed the cat. I come home with flowers. My partner is confused – did I just buy her some flowers to apologise for not feeding the cat? Understanding the spread of the COVID-19 virus is a good example of the need to take time lags into account. During the early stages of the pandemic, some government leaders said the spread was under control because only a handful of cases had been identified. But in a country where ten people had been identified with the virus, there may have been thousands infected. Some people didn't show signs of the virus for 12–14 days, and each of those people likely infected another two to three people during that period.

Positive feedback and exponential cause and effect

Cybernetics models the impact of negative feedback. Systems dynamics also models positive feedback, the effects of which are often exponential, not linear. For example, returning to the spread of COVID-19, at one point in the UK one infected person infected an average of two and a half other people. That doesn't sound like a lot. But if one person infects two and a half people on Monday, those two and a half people will have infected more than six people by Tuesday, who will have infected 16 people by Wednesday, who will have infected 39 people by Thursday. Within two weeks 150,000 people will have become infected from that one initial case.

Causal loops

Imagine an mechanical operations team just barely keeping its head above water. The team receives and processes 100 requests a day, people staying behind if necessary to avoid the build-up of a backlog. Then one day, one member of the team is sick and cannot be replaced. By the end of the day the team has processed only 90 out of the 100 requests, despite some team members staying late. The next day the sick team member is still ill and still cannot be replaced. That same day, 100 new requests come in again. In addition, purveyors of the ten requests that weren't addressed the day before resubmit their requests. Then things start to go seriously wrong in three of those businesses whose requests weren't responded to. This leads to a whole new wave of requests as mechanical issues begin to escalate. Another 50 requests are submitted. The same thing happens on the third day. The team is working so hard that two more team members become sick. The rate of new requests increases exponentially and production has to be completely shut down (Figure 3.1).

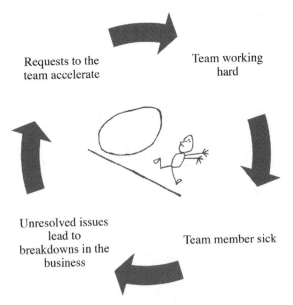

Requests to the team accelerate

Team working hard

Unresolved issues lead to breakdowns in the business

Team member sick

Figure 3.1 Circular causality

With production stopped, the team has time to recuperate. Sick staff get well again and the team gets back to working the way it did before. What no one fully understands is why things got as bad as they did. Surely if one person gets sick, then everyone else needs to work about 10% harder? Why did the system break down so absolutely, so quickly?

This kind of non-linear causality can be hard to spot, so Senge and colleagues identified some common patterns and gave them names. It is hard to hold all these patterns in your head, so people turn to computers to mathematically model these non-linear scenarios. This belief in the power of computers to model the system highlights the similarity between the linear and non-linear ways of thinking about systems. The non-linear perspective recognises a degree of complexity that the linear perspective doesn't. But the underlying premise is the same. The organisation is a system operating according to rules, and those rules, once understood, can be modified and changed by the system designer.

James Miller and living systems theory

James Grier Miller was a psychologist and psychiatrist who worked at Harvard.[1] He suggested that organisations are 'concrete' systems, that can be considered to be living systems. A concrete system must satisfy eight criteria to be called a living system. These include

- The system has open boundaries, able to exchange materials in and out.
- The system can repair itself.
- The system functions according to a blueprint. In the case of an organisation, the blueprint may take the form of processes, charters and constitutions.
- The system contains protoplasm. In an organisation, the protoplasm is the people, flowing around concrete artefacts such as buildings and machines.
- The system must contain a 'decider', who surveys the system and adjusts its function as required.
- Living systems self-regulate, develop and reproduce. They have purposes and goals.

The organisation is viewed as a living system, comprising boundaried sub-systems, all of which interact with each other. Instead of liver, spleen and lungs, the organisation comprises of divisions, each of which is made up of sub-groups, teams and individuals. Living systems theory is different to some of the theories outlined already. It explicitly depicts parts as being interdependent, connected by and subject to ongoing process. The internal system is in a state of constant flux, parts responding not only to each other, but also to events outside the system.

Both systems dynamics and living systems theory are different to linear first order theories in that they recognise the complexity of causal relationships. Looking at the world through a linear lens, I am quick to latch onto nice, simple, cause and effect (e.g. climate change is a perception based on the invention of air conditioning) and take action accordingly. Looking at the world through a systems dynamics or living systems theory lens, I spend time more thoroughly exploring the nature of the system. What all these theories have in common, however, is that they position the organisation as a real system.

Philosophy

A coach thinking through a first order non-linear lens is likely to align to the following perspectives:

1 Perspective on system

The organisation is still a system. Whilst it is recognised that causal links are hard to identify, it can be done. The non-linear perspective doesn't see the organisation as a simple machine. A living system is nearer the mark. A living system consists of component parts, but the relationship between parts is dynamic and ongoing. It *is* a system, with real boundaries separating inside from outside. As a coach working systemically in this mode, I have a pretty sophisticated Wiener Filter, capable of identifying complex cause and effect. I don't make assumptions so quickly. I look beyond A + B = C and look for more complicated patterns. Patterns help me identify causal loops, positive feedback and time lags.

2 Perspective on people

The dual role of the leader remains a feature of this perspective. On the one hand the manager is like everyone else, playing a role as a component in the system. But the manager is also able to step out of the system when she likes, to make changes to the system. The manager is the 'decider'. Through this lens you must have a designer, since everyone else in the system is expected to play a passive role with no real responsibility for innovation or change. The emphasis is on stability and continuity. The coach, again, is a visitor to the system, a neutral bystander with no assigned role to play in the functioning of the system. Again, the role of the coach is to help leaders to work out how best to discharge their decider function.

3 Perspective on change

As before, the system does not change itself purposefully. The system is designed to do what it has been designed to do by the system designer. Maintaining equilibrium is an objective, and discordance is seen as a threat to stability and efficiency. Change can come from two sources. Open boundaries mean that the external environment can pervade the internal environment. If left unchecked, this invasion can trigger mayhem and disruption. The system designer has a guardian angel role to play, monitoring the interaction between internal and external, and making changes where required to maintain the integrity of the system. Purposeful change is still something that is done to a system by the system designer.

4 Perspective on power

Power is still centralised in the system designer. And everyone else in the system is still ultimately expected to perform as decided by the system designer. Positional power remains sacrosanct. The leader needs to be smart, however, capable of working out the complex nature of the system. So, the leader is still a 'great man' ultimately responsible for making good decisions, but this great leader takes time to make decisions, investing more time in system analysis.

5 Perspective on team coaching

As before, an effective team defined through this lens is a team of people with clearly defined roles. The focus remains on ensuring that each person on the team is managing their part of the operation efficiently. Processes are still well defined, and everyone in every function understands their role and set of responsibilities. Links between processes in different functions remain the focus of attention, but it is not assumed that these links are straightforward or easy to understand. The coach here is more likely to look at the functioning of the whole system in order to diagnose a local issue. The leader of the team is still the head designer and so has final say on all decisions.

Purpose

A coach thinking through this lens still spends most of her time with her coachee. She still holds the leader accountable to exercising his individual responsibilities as leader and still believes you can 'change an organisation one person at a time'. The coach's purpose may not be so different to the linear coach, though she likely prides herself more in terms of her capacity to help leaders diagnose and pull apart complex issues.

Practice

Kelly and Allen

The last time Kelly and Allen met, Allen was distressed. His initial attempts to increase sales had apparently been successful. He recruited a new intelligence guy, he trained up some of the new salespeople and he gave Sean and Helen more room to operate. But then sales dropped suddenly. Allen felt compelled to take charge, to manage every detail. The team is miserable and Allen is working long hours. He doesn't show up for a couple of sessions but then calls Kelly up, telling her that he thinks his job may be on the line.

Kelly: What makes you think your job is on the line?
Allen: The CEO pretty much told me. He said that he and the board need to understand why sales have fallen. They want to know what we plan to do about it. I was straight up with him and told him I needed more time. He didn't look pleased. I need to get back to him soon.

Kelly: What do you think is happening?

Allen: It's hard to say. Marketing is coming up with lots of new sales promotions, and each time a new promotion is launched, sales initially go up. But then you get this crash. It's happened twice now.

Kelly: What causes the crash?

Allen: People just stop buying. We've tried surveys, talking to customers. The new market intelligence guy is getting that all organised. Initial feedback suggests we may have problems in the warehouse. Kirsty heads up distribution and I told her she needs to pull her finger out, but she's not being helpful.

Kelly: How isn't she being helpful?

Allen: She says that when orders rise suddenly, without warning, it puts pressure on warehouse staff. She says they're doing their best. I think they just need to get their act together.

Kelly: So, you launch a new promotion, orders go up, something happens in the warehouse, and then sales drop.

Allen: When you put it like that . . . but I can't see how it all connects. Sales do go up after a promotion, so we're obviously delivering. The problem is retaining those customers. We need a new marketing promotion, I think, one that's focussed on existing customers, and that's what I've got Sean looking at now.

Kelly: Hmmm.

Allen: (*Impatient.*) What does 'hmmm' mean?

Kelly: Listening to you, I'm not convinced you've succeeded yet in understanding what's happening. Why would sales fall off a cliff just because you're not running a customer retention programme? Do your competitors run retention programmes?

Allen: No. It would be a first in the market. That's why it's so exciting.

Kelly: Again, listening to you, I'm wondering if you've yet worked out what's going on. You talk about distribution as if it's got nothing to do with you, Kirsty's problem. I'm not hearing what might really be happening there.

Allen: I told you, when we launch a promotion, sales go up.

Kelly: I heard you. I'm just sharing with you what's going on for me as I'm listening to you. I'm curious to see what your market intelligence people come up with. Why have customers stopped buying your product?

Allen: (*Wearily.*) Let me go away and ask more questions.

The week after, Kelly finds Allen looking purposeful and energetic.

Kelly: You look happier today.

Allen: I am happier. I think we now know what's been happening. Look here. (*Allen produces a piece of paper with a diagram on it – Figure 3.2.*). I told you orders went up after each promotion – right?

Kelly: Right.

Allen: And they did. Because warehousing got the first orders out without any problem. But then we got backlogs and, in some cases, product being shipped to the wrong address, etc.

Kelly: How do you know?

Allen: Because I went and visited the warehouse with Kristy. She was only too pleased to show me what was going on. I should have paid more attention earlier.

Kelly: Go on.

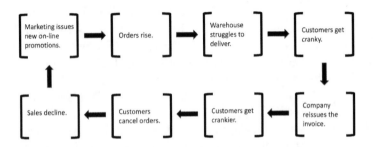

Figure 3.2   Allen's diagram

Allen: Well, the warehouse struggled to deliver, and customers got cranky. But they didn't cancel their orders straightaway. They waited.

Kelly: And then?

Allen: Well that's the interesting bit. Invoicing systems haven't been working properly either. We found this out only after talking to a couple of customers, ex-customers I should say, who just wanted to vent. They might have been waiting three or four weeks for a product, or else received the wrong product and had to send it back. Then they got a letter complaining they hadn't paid their invoice, even though they had.

Kelly: Not good.

Allen: Not good at all, because the wording in some of these letters is quite high-handed. Anyway, sales then fell off the cliff, but both times it was quite a while after the promotion.

Kelly: Even though the promotion kicked it all off?

Allen: Yes, the promotion kicked it all off because the promotion caused people to all buy at once. That put pressure on the system which the system couldn't cope with, but the impact was delayed.

Kelly: And the low sales pushed you to keep launching more promotions, which put even more pressure on the system.

Allen: That's it.

Kelly: What are you doing about it?

Allen: I've mapped it all out with Kristy and we now know exactly what we need to do. We've run analyses that show us how much extra resource we need to put on in warehousing, based on sales forecasts. They've also worked out why product was going to wrong addresses and put that right. And we've both spoken to Finance about the invoicing piece. We've introduced a new algorithm that blocks the sending of an invoice reminder until we have confirmation of delivery. And they've changed the wording.

Kelly: Anything else?

Allen: (*Shakes his head.*) No. I know what's going on now. We have the whole system mapped out and it's all working well. We've got some apologising to do to the customers we upset, and so we have some plans there too.

Kelly: And the new promotion to retain customers?

Allen: Not a priority.

Coaching through this lens

Based on this philosophy, we might expect coaches to behave as described in the following.

1 **Data collection**

The coach thinking through this lens has a keen nose for data. She expects the issue to be complicated and leaves no stone unturned in asking questions about different aspects of the organisation. She has her Wiener Filter turned to 'rigorous analysis' mode, conscious of the risks of making assumptions too quickly. Listening to Allen's story, Kelly heard big holes in the narrative. What was really happening in the warehouse? What does his team still not know out about the customer's experience? Her curiosity encouraged Allen to delve deeper. One technique advocated by Senge and colleagues is the five whys.[2] For example:

1 Why did sales crash? (Because customers were unhappy.)
2 Why were customers unhappy? (Because product was arriving late and they were getting invoice reminders.)
3 Why was product arriving late? (Because the warehouse was experiencing problems.)
4 Why was the warehouse experiencing problems? (Because of a sudden influx of orders.)
5 Why did they experience a sudden influx of orders? (Because we launched new promotions.)

In answering the questions, the responder should avoid assigning blame (e.g. 'because the warehouse is staffed by a bunch of idiots'). This tends to signal the end of curiosity. If the warehouse staff didn't perform as expected, and that's an issue, then ask why they didn't perform as expected?

I recall a real example from my time as a leader working overseas. We hired someone new to manage a particular department. We had important projects lined up and they weren't getting done. This person worked for me, and whenever I asked him about the projects, he assured me they would be soon back on track. But they never were. Then we had this conversation:

1 Why is project X behind schedule? (Because the supplier didn't deliver on time.)
2 Why didn't the supplier deliver on time? (He said he needed more information.)
3 Why did he need more information? (Because there were some gaps in the product brief.)
4 Why were there gaps in the product brief? (Because I prepared it in a hurry.)
5 Why did you prepare it in a hurry? (Because I'm having to squeeze all my work into the afternoon.)
6 Why are you having to squeeze all your work into the afternoon? (Because I'm on email all morning.)
7 Why are you on email all morning? (Because I have emails incoming from overnight from the UK and US that I'm obliged to read.)
8 Why are you obliged to read those emails? (Because in this company I'm obliged to be an active member of the global network and ensure our product design is consistent with global standards.)
9 Why is it taking all morning to read those emails? (Because English is my second language and it takes me a long time to read materials written in English.)

Note that we don't have to stop at five questions. We stop when we think we have found the point of leverage through which we can change the design of the system. In this case, Kelly just got Allen started. After she asked a couple of questions, he understood what she was up to and went and pursued his own line of questioning with Kristy and others.

2   Looking for less obvious causal relationships

A fly on the wall would have seen Kelly focussing furiously as she listened to Allen's story. She didn't accept his first diagnosis of the issue as being the right diagnosis. Through her analytical lens she sensed pieces of the picture Allen hadn't yet addressed, aspects of the system he seemed to be ignoring because he had already decided that Kirsty's incompetence was the cause of the issue. Kelly shared her perspective with Allen and let him do with it as he chose. Of course, he seized upon it. He had spent weeks trying to deal with this issue, without success. What Kelly said made sense. In practice we might see coach and coachee standing at the whiteboard, drawing the system together. Or the coachee might have the pen and the coach might be standing to one side asking questions. Whatever the methodology, the coach is asking questions that invite the coachee to think differently about the issue. The coach encourages the coachee to step up from their immediate assumptions, to consider their dilemma from a new vantage point.

3   Respecting boundaries

The non-linear thinker is no different to the linear thinker in thinking about organisations in terms of boundaries. This is akin to the living systems analogy where there is a boundary between the inside of the system and its environment, and between the different sub-systems in the 'organism'. So, you will find the coach joining the coachee in talking about different levels of the organisation and different functions and teams as if these are real phenomena, a perspective we will see challenged later. If you notice their language, Kelly and Allen are both happy to talk about Marketing and Operations, Distribution and Finance as if they are real entities. Allen is Head of Marketing and Sales and sees Kristy as Head of Distribution. They head up their own separate sub-systems and are responsible for what happens in those systems. Allen has a breakthrough when he asks if he can enter the Distribution sub-system, as a kind of visitor. Kristy is delighted to let him through the door so he can better understand her world. If you were to watch coach and coachee drawing the system on the whiteboard, you would likely see big circles being drawn for each function in the organisation, and a big circle around the functions to represent the boundary dividing the organisation from the rest of the world. The rest of the world can also be divided into subsystems, through the use of acronyms such as PESTLE.[3]

4 Viewing change as a project or programme

This perspective is no different to linear thinking. Kelly and Allen are still seeing the goal as being to increase sales to previous levels, to get back to normal. This implies that Allen's role is to build a stable system. The organisation is still a system, with Allen as system designer trying to work out what design changes he needs to make. By the end of their conversation Allen is happy. He has worked out what changes he needs to make and is confident the system will now function properly again. It will go back to normal. Through this lens coach and coachee focus on the dilemma, assuming that little else is changing in the system; that the natural order is stability.

5 Focussing on the individual

Again, this perspective is no different to first order linear thinking. Kelly still aligns to the 'great man' theory of leadership in which the leader is ultimately accountable for the functioning of his system or sub-system. As a coach she probably also ascribes to the idea that Allen is ultimately capable of achieving whatever he sets his mind to. So, though Allen may need to engage with others in working out the answer to this complicated problem, this is only collaboration of a sort, limited in scope. It is about leveraging other people's brainpower, their capacity to think logically and rationally about a problem. Ultimately, Allen sees it as his responsibility to decide what needs to be done and make sure it happens. Kelly is of the same view, and the two of them will happily work on forming plans that Allen feels confident enacting.

Leading through this lens

A leader with access to this way of thinking is probably more resilient under pressure than the leader with access only to linear thinking. This leader is used to working in situations where there is no obvious solution and is relatively relaxed in that scenario. She can tell you stories, examples from her life, where she and others made quick decisions that turned out to be wrong. She is more inclined to put the brakes on, call a timeout and spend time determining what exactly is going on. This is a leader who values intelligence. The leader remains an advocate of clear objectives, KPIs and job descriptions. The leader still believes in positional power and still expects senior leaders to have the capacity to work things out. She may get frustrated with senior leaders who make hasty decisions without stopping to pull apart complicated issues. The leader spends lots of time mulling over problems and working out solutions.

Developing leaders

The basic philosophy of leadership is no different to before. The organisation is still working from a realist perspective and with the idea that great leaders get great outcomes as they become more skilled at pulling the right levers. Those levers may be related to task or to people. Motivating people is still regarded as a skill to be learned to ensure people do what they are supposed to do while staying happy and engaged. The programme may feature a section on 'systems thinking', where systems thinking is the logical, rational analysis of the organisation and its environment as a real system. This capacity to think systemically (as defined) may become a required leadership skill, part of the competency framework, at least for senior leaders.

It is in the arena of leadership development that we perhaps most need a new language for talking about systems thinking. Most organisations talk about complexity and uncertainty and recognise the need for leaders to behave differently. For many this means simply standing back, taking a holistic view, recognising how complicated the world can be and teaching much the same content in much the same way. As we will see in the next few chapters, different perspectives on system seed different approaches to content, format and strategy.

At the movies

Groundhog Day is a good movie to watch in thinking about the difference between linear and non-linear causality. Weatherman Phil Connors visits Punxsutawney with news producer Rita Hanson and cameraman Larry to cover the Groundhog Day festivities on February 2. At the beginning of the film Phil is depicted as a cynical, even nasty person, with no time for others. Except for Rita, who he would like to take to bed. The three of them film the Groundhog Day ceremony and prepare to return to Pittsburgh, but there is a snowstorm and they have to spend the night in Punxsutawney. The next morning, Phil wakes up and it is the morning of February 2 again. The day plays itself out exactly as it did the day before. Phil goes to bed and again wakes up on February 2, and again, and again. Every day is Groundhog Day. Phil spends the next few Groundhog Days eating, drinking, having sex and generally indulging himself. Then he becomes depressed and tries to kill himself. But he still keeps waking up on February 2. Phil remains the same person, trying out different strategies to try to change the outcome, all to no avail. His first order linear thinking doesn't work. Then Phil opens himself to the possibility that the 'hicks' who inhabit Punxsutawney might be good people. He opens himself up to the possibility that those people might help him to become a better person. Now we have a causal loop. What Phil does impacts on the people of the town, and how the people of the town respond to Phil, changes Phil. One day Phil tells Rita he loves her, because he really does. He finally awakens on the morning of February 3.

In organisations we see this phenomenon play itself out. The term 'Groundhog Day' has become part of the everyday vernacular. Same problems, same solutions, same failure to address. Some problems are obviously complex. Simple linear cause-and-effect thinking doesn't work. People recognise that they will need to spend some time working out what is going on and how to solve the dilemma. Senior leaders feel compelled to take the time required to work out what's happening.

Your 3Ps

Again, I hope you find yourself wondering, 'And what's wrong with the way Kelly is coaching here?' Remember, these different ways of thinking are not necessarily sequential in the sense that we move lock, stock and barrel from one to the other. Rather, we are developing access to a portfolio of different thinking styles, and the first order non-linear style may serve us well in some contexts.

Some more questions for you:

1 At the beginning of this chapter we considered Senge's theory of systems dynamics and living systems theory. What was *useful* about those two theories?
2 If you review your Purpose again now, has it changed at all? Can it be further refined?
3 What insights have you gained as to how you currently coach now – what is your Practice?
4 Do you coach differently in different contexts? If so, what triggers you in each context?
5 Do you have a glimpse yet of what other practical approaches you might seek to integrate in your practice?

Segue . . .

Allen calls Kelly up two weeks later.

Kelly: Hi, Allen.
Allen: Sales are down again.
Kelly: Straight to the point as always.
Allen: Yes, how are you? You're well? Good. Sales are down.
Kelly: Why are they down this time?
Allen: I don't know. It's an absolute mystery. We've tracked all our processes throughout the entire organisation. It's all working fine. But something's going on.
Kelly: And you've no idea what's happened?
Allen: None whatsoever. When can you come around? I might need to get you in front of the team and help them too. Everyone's got a bit defensive and no one's

      talking to each other. I need people talking to each
      other.

Kelly: OK. I'll see you tomorrow then.

Time for some supervision first, thought Kelly.

Notes

1 Duncan, D.M. (1972). James G. Miller's Living Systems Theory:
  Issues for Management Thought and Practice. *Academy of Management Journal, 15*(4), 513–523.
2 Senge, P., Kleiner, A., Roberts, C., Ross, R. & Smith, B. (1994). *The
  Fifth Discipline Fieldbook.* Doubleday.
3 PESTLE stands for Political, Economic, Sociological, Technological, Legal and Environmental.

4

Second order thinking

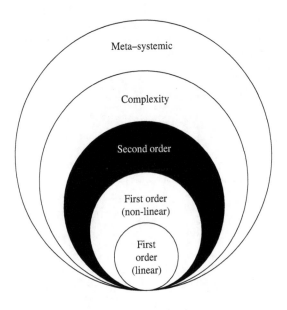

Theory in a nutshell

Gregory Bateson, Peter Checkland and Soft Systems Methodology

Gregory Bateson was a social scientist and anthropologist. He believed that the major problems in the world are a consequence of Man's distorted view of his own capacity to understand complexity.[1] Man looks at complexity, believes he understands the root cause and takes action. Those actions can have disastrous consequences.

For example, the sugar cane industry in Queensland, Australia, was threatened by the proliferation of white grubs in the early 20th century. The grubs ate the roots of the cane, causing it to die. Chemical insecticides, soil fumigation and biocontrol measures didn't work. A government entomologist called Reginald Mungomery imported cane toads from abroad, convinced introduction of the toad would solve the problem, as it had apparently done in Hawaii,  the Philippines and Puerto Rico. In less than two months the number of toads had increased 24-fold. The cane toad soon became a serious problem. It preyed on native fauna, competed for food and carried diseases that were transmitted to frogs and fish. The cane toads ate birds' eggs, killed native frogs and, because its skin is poisonous, killed would-be predators. The toll on native species has been immense. And it didn't have much impact on the white grub because the white grub lived at the top of the sugar cane where the cane toad couldn't reach it. Man was sure he knew the answer, and Man was wrong.

Conflict and war arise when people adopt simplistic perspectives on an issue and debate with each other, each convinced they are right. For example, George believes global warming is a consequence of the rising popularity of air conditioning. Convinced he is right, he sets out on a mission to tell everyone that global warming is a fiction. Meanwhile, Manchester has three days of warm sunshine for the first time in 50 years, and Susan is convinced this must be because of global warming. She sets out on a mission to persuade everyone to take action immediately. George and Susan engage in heated debate.

Bateson was much impressed by the work of Warren McCulloch, another scientist, who studied the optic nervous systems of frogs. McCulloch demonstrated that what the frog sees is limited by the design of its optic system. A frog sees what moves. If a thing doesn't move, the frog doesn't perceive it and, for the frog, it doesn't exist. We are the same. We perceive what we are able to perceive, and what we perceive we regard as a universal reality.

This idea, that people's perceptions are utterly subjective, that there exist multiple truths, is one of three key ideas underpinning Soft Systems Methodology (SSM).[2] Peter Checkland, the primary driver behind the development of SSM, believed that attempts to identify general rules, rules that can be mathematically modelled and applied to all systems, fail. They fail because the world is too "complex, problematical and mysterious"[3] The three core ideas behind SSM are:

1 People are forever trying to define the problems they face so they can work out what action to take.
2 We all interpret the world differently. So, if we are to tackle problems together, we need to compare our perspectives on the system and build a collective perspective.
3 We learn about the system through doing and reflecting on that doing.

A Soft Systems Methodology entails getting people together to compare their perspectives of a problem, to develop a common understanding of the system and to collectively agree on desired change and actions. The emphasis is on the collective, because it is recognised that every individual perspective is subjective and incomplete. 'Rich picture' analysis is a practice that has emerged from soft systems thinking. A rich picture is a visual depiction of the system drawn by a group of people.

If, for example, Allen was to approach his sales problem through this lens, he would be out and about seeking to understand others' perspectives of the problem. Not in service of building engagement per se, but because he recognises how subjective is his view of events. He would truly believe in the importance of soliciting other perspectives if he is to get close to understanding the reality of the whole. He might bring people together to discuss their observations and to build a composite picture of what is going on exactly.

Even that composite view he would regard as hypothetical, one to be tested by doing something and reflecting on the outcome of that action.

The essence of the second order perspective is a realisation that there always exist multiple perspectives on an issue, and that every perspective is equally valid and equally flawed. Put another way, it recognises that we all look at the world through our own personal Weiner Filters, goggles we can never remove. We need to understand what the world looks like through everyone's goggles if we are going to build between us a view of what the world might actually look like.

Philosophy

A coach thinking about systems through a second order lens is likely to align to the following perspectives:

1 Perspective on system

The organisation is still regarded as a real system. Whilst the first order thinker endeavours to find out how the system actually works, the second order thinker endeavours to find out how the system *might* be working. Organisations are always too complex for us to understand, impossible to understand in any 'real' sense, because we are each burdened by the subjectivity of our perceptions. We are stuck with our Wiener Filters. We can never then claim to understand the organisation-as-system as it really is. We can only experience the organisation-as-if-it-were a system, a hypothetical system we envisage in our minds. The coach sees herself and others as frogs, each frog looking at the world through a different lens. Some frogs can see hills and mountains; others can't. Some frogs see the grass blowing in the breeze; others don't. Some frogs see clouds gathering overhead and realise it is about to rain; others don't. As coach, whilst I am forming my own ideas as to the nature of the organisation and how it operates, I am aware that I too am missing things; I am a frog. My coachee is a frog too, a frog looking at the world through a different lens. He is confident he can see the organisation-as-system for what it is. But his version of the system is different to mine. I don't accept his version as gospel, nor I do accept my version as gospel. I am interested in sharing perspectives and trying to see what he sees that I don't, and bringing to his attention what I see that he doesn't. The organisation is a system, but it is impossible to see the design of the system directly. In practical terms we are dealing with organisation-as-story, our *stories* as to the nature of the system. The functioning of the system is a hypothesis, and we must test our hypothesis through taking action and reflecting on the consequences. This philosophy recognises the inevitability of ambiguity, and it encourages curiosity and exploration. Our Wiener Filters are firmly in place, but we take what we see with a pinch of salt.

2 Perspective on people

The biggest difference between first and second order perspectives is that the second order perspective recognises the fallibility of individual perception. It explicitly recognises that we all look at life through our own personal Wiener Filters. This belief compels us to enquire how others view the world.

For example, Bob and Susan are sales executives. Today they have a meeting with Allen, an important client. Susan sits next to Allen, and Bob sits opposite, on the other side of the table. After the meeting, Bob and Susan meet up to compare notes. Bob says he thinks Allen was in an unusually decisive mood. He encouraged Bob and Susan to make their points quickly and he expressed his opinions concisely and clearly. Something must have happened to free him from his habitual fog of ambiguity and uncertainty. He was a pleasure to talk to. By contrast, Susan says she felt uncomfortable. Allen seemed terse and uptight. She saw him holding his hands tightly. He wasn't prepared to talk options like he usually was. He wasn't listening. He just told them to do as they were told. He was evidently under pressure from above and they would have to work hard to maintain a good working relationship.

Which story is 'true'? Bob and Susan don't get into a debate. They are each acutely aware of the limitations of their individual perceptions, and keen to understand the perspective of the other. They swap Wiener Filter experiences. They compare notes, each making an effort to acknowledge what they may have not seen or may have overlooked. They are interested in co-creating a joint hypothesis as to what took place. Only once they have agreed a hypothesis do they decide together what to do next.

Thinking second order, I know I am a frog. And everyone else is a frog too, a different frog. The unaware frog over-privileges his limited perspective and calls it 'reality'. You may have seen the Invisible Gorilla video. Before watching the video, you are told to focus on a basketball being thrown about by a group of people and to count how many times the ball changes hands. In the meantime, a gorilla walks slowly across the basketball court. Many of us are astonished to be told about the gorilla afterwards. We don't see it because we are focussed on the basketball. We don't see it, and so it doesn't exist. Some people refuse to acknowledge the gorilla even after being shown the video a second time. They believe they have been shown two different videos. We see what we are looking for, and we miss what we are not looking for. We focus on what we think we need to focus on, and we are already hypothesising what it is we are looking at. Perception is an active process. When we see a yellow flash in the corner of our eye when walking through a field, we see a flower. Even if it's a crisp packet. Data from the outside world meets our theory as to what is happening in the world, somewhere in the middle. Our perceptions are shaped by previous experience and beliefs. Our perceptions are in no sense unadulterated or objective. We are built to decide quickly what is happening in our environment. We are built to make assumptions. If we didn't, then it would take all day to get to work. It would take me half an hour to step outside my front door, confronted by a myriad of colour, movement, sound and smell. If we think second order, then we recognise that people make assumptions, all the time. The coach listens to the coachee's story forever listening for assumptions and the impact of those assumptions on the coachee's thinking and behaviour.

Ladder of inference

The 'ladder of inference' is a well-known model developed by Chris Argyris to illustrate how people jump to conclusions (Figure 4.1).[4] When we walk into a room, we don't scan for all available data and sift through it logically. We look out for what we expect to see.

For example, John is a leader who *believes* that people need to be closely monitored, otherwise they don't work hard. During COVID-19 he was compelled to ask his team to all work from home. If you had been able to watch each of his staff members in action, each minute of the day, you would have seen that they started work earlier and finished later, because they didn't have to commute. This was the *observable data*. Some of the team took a while to get used to setting their own agenda, without John being there to tell them what to do, but everyone

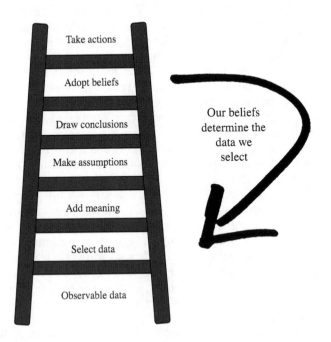

Figure 4.1 Ladder of inference

adapted. They were more productive than they had been before lockdown, though this didn't show up directly in the sales figures, because many of their clients were forced to scale down operations. Whenever John called one of his team, they always seemed busy, but he didn't trust that they weren't pulling the wool over his eyes. Rob is one of John's employees. He and his partner found lockdown challenging, in that they needed to make time to home-school their children. They put aside two hours in the afternoon to spend with their children, adjusting their work time accordingly. One day John called Rob during the middle of a home-schooling session. One of Rob's children answered his video call, and John saw Rob lying on his lounge room floor playing with his two other children. To John, this *meant* that Rob was spending much of his workday playing with his children. He therefore *assumed* that Rob wasn't committed to his work and *concluded* that he would need to get the team back into the office as soon as possible. The whole episode served to further reinforce his *belief* that people couldn't be trusted to work without close supervision. As soon as he was able, he *took action*; he mandated that people return to working in the office, even though many of his staff believed home working helped them perform more efficiently and effectively.

If the coach wants to see the world the way his coachee sees the world, then he needs to pay attention to the mental model through which she is viewing the world. When the coachee talks about coming into conflict with others, the coach will likely find himself thinking about the disagreement as a clash of mental models. And he recognises that he is thinking through a mental model of his own and is interested how his mental model is determining what data he is listening and responding to.

Once we acknowledge our inability to experience reality directly, then the limitations of individual perception are constantly apparent. I will not cite the names of particular politicians in this book, nor do I need to. You will all have your favourite examples of people who respond to grand events with simple mantras, mantras they cling on to tightly for fear of being seen as wishy-washy or irresolute. Political boundaries are drawn and politicians squabble like schoolchildren from either side of the wall, neither side attempting for a moment to understand the value of the other perspective. It is perhaps this constant bickering that leads many of us to feel so weary listening to politicians talking. A tired despair that none of them seem to be interested in understanding how others think.

Yet in the coaching room, how often do we rely upon our coachee's telling of a story? Or our perception of their story? If perception is subjective and fallible by design, then we must be wary of depending on single perceptions of events. We must recognise the limitations of our own perceptions, the perceptions of our coachees and the perceptions of our fellow coaches and supervisors. The second order thinker sees people as highly subjective, subject to their own mental models.

Nevertheless, the second order thinker shares the same dualism as does the first order thinker. The second order thinker recognises the limitations of his perception and seeks to understand the views of others. He is inclusive. But he still believes he can be both the system designer and part of the system. He may invite others to come look at the system with him, not just the coach, to sit observe and share perspectives, but this vantage is still external. Others in the system don't enjoy the same privilege. They are part of the system only, and the system designer can still intervene and change the design of the system without their involvement. There is still an underlying belief in the capacity of the leader to diagnose situations and control outcomes. The process is just a bit more hit-and-miss.

3 Perspective on change

Nothing fundamental has changed here. Responsibility for the functioning of the system still sits with the (collaborative) system designer. The second order thinker is not quite the same 'great man' as the first order thinker, capable of discerning how the system works and coming up with effective action plans through rational excellence.

The greatness of the second order thinker lies in her curiosity and willingness to understand others' perspectives. But still, there remains a belief in the power of personal agency. It is for the leader to take action and to reflect on the outcomes of that action. The leader still seeks to control the direction of the organisation, if not through 'command and control', then through a more facilitative and collaborative process[5] and through taking action and reflecting on outcomes. The second order coach believes in learning through doing. This is a different twist to the first order approach, in which the coachee comes up with committed actions, then reflects with the coach during the next session as to what happened and what to do next. The second order coach's experimentation is wider in scope, with reflection always including a reflection on the nature of the system, not just the coachee's experiences within that system.

4 Perspective on power
Power is still centralised in the system designer, though the system designer may be more inclusive and benevolent. The leader is still a 'great man' ultimately responsible for making good decisions, but this great leader actively solicits the views and perspectives of others.

5 Perspective on team coaching
This team is more curious about the world around it and less definitive around role and job description. The world is always ambiguous and uncertain, and so roles and job descriptions need to be more flexible. Indeed, the team may not bother putting roles and job descriptions into written format; they may be more a focus of ongoing conversation. Conversation between team members is likely more dialogic and enquiring. Everyone on the team is aware of their own limitations and less inclined to a strictly siloed approach in which everyone concerns themselves primarily with their own functions. Team coaching is likely to include more work on team dynamics, since team members place greater emphasis on their capacity to relate effectively. The team may also be more attentive to their relationships with other stakeholders. Other stakeholder perspectives are of real interest because the team is aware

of the risk of over-investing in its own collective view as to how the organisation is functioning in its environment.

Purpose

A coach thinking through a second order lens still holds the leader accountable to exercising his individual responsibilities as leader and still believes you can 'change an organisation one person at a time'. The coach sees part of her role as encouraging people in an organisation to collaborate with each other to compare perspectives on issues, engaging in collective problem solving.

Practice

Kelly and Allen

Kelly spoke to a supervisor before meeting with Allen again. She explained how Allen seems to have exhausted his options in terms of mapping out the system and finding leverage points. Her supervisor introduced her to second order ways of thinking about systems. Kelly understood the theory and realised it might be useful were Allen able to access some fundamentally different ways of thinking about his predicament. She thought about calling him up beforehand to suggest that instead of convening his team, he brings together a more diverse group of people. She decided against it. She decided she needed to work with Allen's current frame of reference rather than look to impose her own.

She goes to Allen's office as arranged and enters a room full of people: Allen and his six direct reports. Allen introduces everyone and explains to the team that Kelly is his coach. He explains that the purpose of the meeting is to further explore the decline in sales and then invites people to speak. Everyone sits quietly. Kelly senses people watching her.

Kelly: Allen, perhaps you might explain why you asked me to be here.

Allen: Ah. Yes. Well I invited Kelly here today because she's been helping me over the last few months. She helped me see that I was being too hands-on. And helped me understand how I don't always invest enough energy in exploring problems. It was her questions that encouraged me to go and talk to Kristy. I've asked her to come today to help us all to explore the latest fall-off in sales. I'm stuck, frankly, and everyone else seems stuck too. (*The room falls quiet again.*)

Kelly: What do you all think might be going on?

Sean: It's not a warehousing problem. Distribution swear blind they're handling all the orders now.

Rob: (*The new market intelligence guy.*) The customers we've spoken to say the same thing. No problems with deliveries or orders.

Kelly: What else do customers say?

Rob: The only negative comment is price. Recently some customers have been saying our shoes are expensive. But it's only a proportion of customers and we've checked pricing. Nothing's happened in the market, no one's discounting. So, it can't be that.

Kelly: What could it be?

(*Long silence*)

The way I'm asking the question maybe sounds like I'm expecting you to come up with well-thought-through, solid theories. I'm not. I'm just asking you to share whatever might be on your mind. No idea too silly.

Sean: A public vendetta designed to lose us all our jobs.

Rob: A sudden switch in public taste.

Helen: Yes, everyone's wearing flippers this year.

Allen: Plastic is the new leather. (*More silence.*)

Kelly: Can I make a suggestion?

Allen: Please.

Kelly: You're the leadership team. You're of similar ages, sort of. You've spent a lot of time in each other's company. You're all male, except for Helen. You probably all read the same newspapers and watch the same TV shows.

Allen: Are you saying we're stuck in groupthink?

Kelly: Sort of. I'm not saying you have no diversity in the team. I'm saying that you seem to have exhausted all options in working out what to do next. You've pulled apart the system, redesigned it and put it back together again. But sales are still falling. Something is happening out there, and none of you can see it. Perhaps there are folk out there who look at life differently to you, who can see what you can't see.

Helen: One of those Millennials.

Kelly: Who might you talk to? (*The team members all look at each other.*)

A week later Kelly was again invited to the team meeting. The team were all present, as were two confident looking young people.

Kelly: Hello again.

Helen: Hello, Kelly. These are members of my team. They don't report directly to me, but I've brought them along today because they told me something I had no clue about. Lucy and Martin.

Allen: And we're waiting on tenterhooks to hear what they have to say.

Helen: Go on, Lucy.

Lucy: Cool. Well I know you guys are all wondering why sales have gone down. I assume you tune into social media? (*The management team members look at each other as if to say, 'Who's got time?'*)

Lucy: (*Looks doubtfully at Martin, then at Helen, then turns to the team.*) Which media do you subscribe to? (*No one replies.*)

Helen: Tell them about the song.

Lucy: People are complaining about the price of Shoozon shoes.

Allen: (*Looks to Rob.*) But we looked at that. Our prices haven't changed.

Lucy: Prices might not have changed, but there's still a song. A customer rang up a store and complained and recorded the conversation on her phone.

Allen: Is that legal?

Lucy: (*Shrugs.*) Anyway she was only 16 or something, and the store manager was pretty rude. He told her to bog off if she didn't like his shoes.

Allen: (*Mystified.*) *Bog* off?

Lucy: Yes. Then she took the recording and set it to the tune of 'Damn Right I've Got the Blues'.

Allen: What's that?

Lucy: It's a really old song. By someone called Buddy Guy. The original version starts 'You damn right, I've got the blues. From my head down to my shoes'. Her version goes 'You damn right, I've got the blues. Bog off if you don't like my shoes' with the shop-guy's voice saying the last bit.

Martin: (*Grinning.*) It is *really* funny. It went viral. Over 250,000 likes so far.

Allen: (*Grim faced.*) Which store was it?

Lucy: (*Shrugs again.*) No idea. But the word is all our store managers are rude.

Allen: (*Looks to Helen.*) We haven't heard that before, have we?

Helen: No. But then we haven't really focussed on the teen market before. They're not our main customer segment.

Lucy: It's not only teens on social media.

Allen: We need to do something.

Rob: But what if this is just a red herring? We're going to go off and assume it's true? Isn't that what we did before?

Allen: I'm not assuming it's true, Rob. If we had lots of other theories to choose from, then we could spend some time sifting through them. I do intend to go and talk to other people and hear more perspectives, I think we all should. One thing I'm learning today is we need to understand the customer's voice a lot better. There may be lots going on we don't know about. But let's get on and test this idea out in the meantime. I don't know if it's true, but let's treat it as a hypothesis, do something and see what happens. Whatever happens, we'll learn something.

After the meeting Helen and Lucy went straight into action. They hired the services of a well-known social media company, who responded to the clip by producing a new clip of their own, responding with humour and grace while letting people know that Shoozon had revised their pricing policy ('You damn right, I've got the blues. Had to cut the price of all my shoes'). Sales slowly recovered.

Coaching through this lens

Again, bear in mind there is no such thing as a second order coach. We are each on our own journey, continually exploring different ways of thinking in different contexts. The question here is not a binary one – is this you, or is it not you? The question is, to what extent do you identify with the approach described, and when is it effective?

1 Respecting systems

Like the first order coach, the second order coach still talks about the organisation as if it is a system. She pays attention to the boundaries of the organisation and makes a clear distinction between those inside the organisation and those outside. The organisation can still usefully be compared to a system, even if the functioning of the system is complex and mysterious. All data is still useful.

2 Encouraging the coachee to seek out others' perspectives

A traditional coaching model says that the role of the coach is to help the coachee work out answers to their own dilemmas. The coach asks questions in service of helping the coachee shape his own perspective. The coach respects the coachee's perspective as a suitable frame from which to move forward. The second order coach regards the coachee's viewpoint as always valid and always incomplete. Such a coach is likely to poke and prod the coachee into exploring other perspectives, particularly the perspectives of people in remote parts of the system. The coach offers her perspective, not with any expectation that the coachee will hear their perspective as 'truth', but as just one of multiple perspectives that ought to enrich the coachee's ultimate interpretation of events. Offering a subjective perspective is different to speaking with certainty, and the coach is happy if her viewpoint is rejected.

3 Holding it lightly
The world of the first order coach is logical and rational. It is a world in which inhabitants seek comfort in the idea that systems can be designed and tweaked and outcomes controlled. Uncertainty induces stress because it implies we have failed in our efforts to control. The world of the second order coach is implicitly dark and mysterious. Efforts to map out the system accurately and in great detail may be wasted. Uncertainty and ambiguity are inevitable. They are a feature of the world rather than a symptom of our failings. If leader and coach believe the world is complex and mysterious, and they happily acknowledge their own limitations in being able to discern the functioning of the system, then they are more likely to hold their perspectives as hypothesis. In other words, the coach is more likely to hold lightly her understanding of the organisation and its boundaries. She holds lightly her coachee's perspective and the reported perspectives of others in his world. She neither welcomes nor rejects ambiguity. Ambiguity just is.

4 Creating new perspectives together
'Rich picturing' is a technique borne of SSM and other second order systems thinking. When one looks back at the conversation Allen and his team had, it would be very easy for individual perspectives to go unheard or to be only half understood. The conversation once finished is complete, and difficult for others to build on. Had they gathered round a whiteboard, they could have drawn their

viewpoints together. Drawing perspectives makes them easier to see and understand, makes them easy to retain and makes it easier for everyone to see the connections between perspectives. In this way a group of people can build up a rich picture of any scenario, rich in detail, but also rich in diversity. In their short conversation, Allen and his team might have come up with something like the picture in Figure 4.2. The team can come back and refer back to their picture later. They can build on it and change it and can share it with others.

We said that the first order non-linear coach might take to the whiteboard too. But what's happening at this whiteboard is different. The first order non-linear coach sees the process as one that helps the leader work out for himself what is happening in the system. The second order coach encourages groups of people to come together to draw a picture that incorporates different perspectives. The second order coach feels happy about picking up a pen herself and joining in.

5 Exploring mental models

Multiple perspectives come from multiple vantage points and multiple beliefs as to how the world operates. If one person tells me that the organisation in which they work is 'toxic' and another person in the same organisation tells me it is 'robustly competitive', it doesn't seem particularly useful to decide which perspective is 'true'. Whatever process I deploy to decide which perspective is 'true' will not tell me which perspective is true; it will tell me only what perspective is true for me. Expressing what is true for me is often a useful thing to do, because adding my viewpoint to the mix is enriching. But in my role as coach, seeking to help people attain a more holistic perspective on the system in which they are operating, I must simultaneously be able to rise above my viewpoint and see it as one of many. So, when person A tells me the organisation is 'toxic', I am interested in understanding what that means, and what behaviours may accompany that perspective.

If I like the ladder of inference as a framework, I might ask the person to help me understand in what way the organisation is toxic. In listening to the answer to my ques-

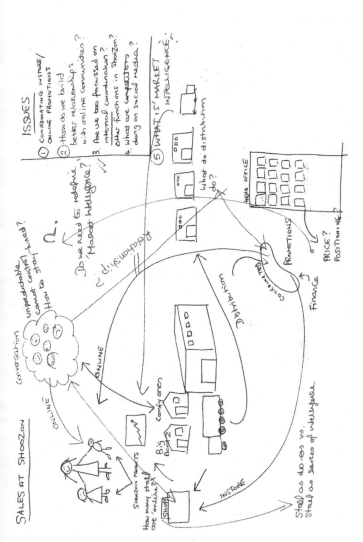

Figure 4.2 Sales at Shoozon

tion, I can hear what data and experiences the person is attending to. I can get a sense of what data is not being attended to, what events may have been overlooked. I can get a sense of how particular events are translating into meanings and assumptions and conclusions. For example, the person tells me the story of a manager who took a comment from one of his direct reports made in a development conversation and used it against her in a performance evaluation. When talking about her development, she said she didn't feel confident answering difficult questions posed to her by customers. At her performance review, her manager told her that she needed to be more confident answering difficult questions if she was to get a better performance rating. The person telling this story gets angry as she recounts it. I hear her talk about her manager's lack of courage and integrity. She assumes he is duplicitous and untrustworthy. She concludes that the organisation is happy for managers to behave in this way, which only goes to reinforce her belief that organisations don't care about their people, that all they care about is financial outcomes. I recognise the person I'm talking to is on the lookout for more such stories, the telling of which will reinforce her existing assumptions and beliefs. If this person is my coachee, then I might share my experience of the conversation. I might share some stories of my own, events I have witnessed in the organisation that appear not to support her hypothesis. I don't do this because I think I am right and she is wrong. I do it because it may help her catch a glimpse of her mental model and alert her to the value of other perspectives.

Two people sharing the same vantage point may still interpret events differently because they are wearing different Wiener Filters. For example, Donald and Emma are colleagues. Donald used to work for a travel company where people always expressed their views after taking their time to reflect. Feedback was always thoughtful and non-judgemental. True, the world moves quickly and sometimes people forgot to give the feedback at all or just found it all too hard, but the culture was ultimately respectful. Here, people seem to say whatever comes into their mind regardless of hurting others' feelings. This is a 'toxic' place to work. Emma also used to work for a travel company. In her travel company, people were direct with each other to the point of bluntness. Sometimes people didn't manage their emotions very well and delivered their message with anger and finger-pointing. Emma appreciated that work environment because she always knew where she stood. She didn't feel threatened by others' anger, because she knew it was all about context. Those same people who got angry were always friendly outside of work, with a beer in hand. What Emma can't stand is people who don't get to the point, talk about others behind their back and slow things down. *That* would be a toxic organisation. This organisation is 'robustly competitive' and a good place to work.

As coach I'm interested in understanding these different mental models because it helps me understand the difference between what is happening and people's interpretations of what is happening. It helps me watch out for assumptions and the nature of assumptions different people tend to make.

Leading through this lens

The leader coaching through a second order still expects others to achieve specific outcomes within specific timeframes. She may still demonstrate a commitment to ensuring all staff have clear objectives, KPIs and a job description. She may still hold strong views based on individual accountability and hold high expectations of more senior leaders to sort out issues according to their pay grade. At the same time, this leader recognises that things often don't go to plan. This is only to be expected given the inherent complexity of organisations. The second order leader likely shows up as unusually curious as to what others are thinking and why. She may make more time in her meetings for people to reflect together. She may willingly and carefully engage in 'office politics', spending time getting out and about to understand others' points of view. We hear these leaders talk about the importance of control, personal accountability and responsibility, and we hear the importance of collaboration and respect for others.

Developing leaders

The purpose of programmes designed through this lens remains to remind the leader of their responsibilities and to provide them with tools and frameworks to discharge those responsibilities most effectively. There are some differences though. Programme designers recognise that different leaders think differently and that there is validity in those differences, within parameters. Programme designers recognise that the organisation is complex and that the leader must exercise judgement in diagnosing a scenario and choosing how to respond. As a consequence, there is likely to be more emphasis on reflection. Assuming the programme is workshop-based, those workshops are less likely to be overstuffed with models and frameworks. Participants will be afforded more time to make sense of the material for themselves, talking to others in the group and exploring the diversity of perspective contained within the group. This time is regarded as necessary to help people work out how to apply new insights in their own individual, complex environments. Programme facilitators are less likely to play the role of subject-matter experts and are more likely to engage people in working out their own answers. Budgets permitting, participants are likely to be afforded a coach, to help them think through issues. Senior leaders may make an appearance. They are less likely to give rousing speeches about how to be a great leader, and more likely to engage in dialogue, recognising that the individual leader, ultimately, needs to work out how to have the greatest impact in their particular scenario. We are still in a world where the purpose of leadership development is to teach employees how to exercise disciplinary power, but it is recognised that different approaches are required to manage different scenarios.

At the movies

The second movie featured in the paper by Harri Raisio and Niklas Lundstrom is *Chaos Theory*. It's interesting in that it really doesn't talk to chaos theory at all. It might be better titled *Second Order Systems Theory*, though that wouldn't be as catchy. Frank, the central character, is a lecturer on time management. He lives by example, planning out his days to the last minute. One day his wife changes the clocks by ten minutes so that Frank can get up ten minutes earlier and do a task for her without having to replan his whole day. Unfortunately, she accidentally sets the clocks ten minutes later instead of earlier. Frank cannot cope. He misses the ferry to work and the rest of his day is ruined. The whole system falls over. One consequence of this disastrous day is that Frank finds out he is not the biological father of his daughter. Feeling betrayed and that he has wasted his life, he abandons the straight and narrow and decides to subject himself to fate. His faith in the sanctity of the system has been destroyed. Like the Dice Man in the book by Luke Rhinehart,[6] he makes decisions by choosing one of three index cards at random.

Old Frank believed that A + B leads to C, and that he was in control of his life. Upon discovering that he wasn't in control of his life at all, he experiences a fundamental failure of faith in his capacity to design a meaningful new system. Instead he relates to life as a mysterious black box. There is no discerning how it works, and so there is no point in trying to live life logically. Instead he comes up with actions at random and sees what happens next. Of course, his actions are not really random at all. Each time he makes a choice, he is choosing from predetermined options he has come up with himself. His range of options is therefore limited by his own capacity to come up with options. This is not quite SSM because Frank is coming up with the options on his own. If he were in cahoots with a friend, then we would have SSM in action.

Your 3Ps

Similar questions to before:

1 What was useful about the second order perspective?
2 If you review your Purpose again now, has it changed at all? Can it be further refined?

3 What insights have you gained as to how you coach now –
   your Practice?
4 Do you coach differently in different contexts? If so, what
   triggers you in each context?
5 Do you have a glimpse yet of what other practical
   approaches you might seek to integrate in your practice?

Segue . . .

Allen and his team came up with a new plan that was
approved by the executive team. As forecast, sales from
physical outlets continue to decline, albeit at a slow rate,
while online sales initially grew at an equivalent to 6% per
annum. Then in July, online sales suddenly took off, jumping 20% overnight. Warehouse stocks were quickly depleted,
the company was unable to meet demand, complaints soared
and the executive team wanted to know why Allen hadn't
done a better job forecasting sales. Did he have a clue what
he was doing? Allen called Kelly.

Allen: We still don't know what triggered it. Sales have
           settled now at a new level about 10% above where
           they were before, which is great, but it would have
           been a lot better had we known it was coming. It was
           just completely random.
Kelly: What theories do you have?
Allen: None whatsoever. Not even Lucy has a theory, and
           she has a theory for everything.
Kelly: Well, at least sales are up.
Allen: Sure, but what if it happens again? If demand lifts
           again, unpredictably, then we get caught with insuf-
           ficient stock. If we increase stock and it doesn't hap-
           pen again, then we have to discount. The executive
           team wants comfort that I know what I'm doing.
           Otherwise they'll start to wonder if we're missing
           out on even more sales growth and go looking for
           someone smarter than me. But what sense am I
           supposed to make of something so random? Things

are just chaotic at the moment. What if sales take a huge *dive* and I can't explain it?

Notes

1 Kobayashi, V.N. (1988). The Self-Reflexive Mind: The Life's Work of Gregory Bateson. *Qualitative Studies in Education, 1*(4), 347–359. "Man" is used to indicate the human species, as per Bateson's terminology.
2 A few to choose from, including Checkland, P. (1994). Systems Theory and Management Thinking. *The American Behavioral Scientist, 38*(1), 756–791; Checkland, P. (2000). Soft Systems Methodology: A Thirty Year Retrospective. *Systems Research and Behavioral Science, 17*, S11–S58; Checkland, P. (2012). Four Conditions for Serious Systems. *Systems Research and Behavioral Science, 29*, 465–469; Checkland, P. & Haynes, M. (1994). Varieties of Systems Thinking: The Case of Soft Systems Methodology. *Systems Dynamics Review, 2/3*, 189–197.
3 Checkland, P. (2000). Soft Systems Methodology: A Thirty Year Retrospective. *Systems Research and Behavioral Science, 17*, S11–S58.
4 There are lots of references. For example, Senge, P., Kleiner, A., Roberts, C., Ross, R. & Smith, B. (1994). *The Fifth Discipline Fieldbook*. Doubleday.
5 Stacey, R.D. & Mowles, C. (2016). *Strategic Management and Organisational Dynamics*, 7th edition. Pearson.
6 Rhinehart, L. (1971). *The Dice Man*. HarperCollins.

Complexity

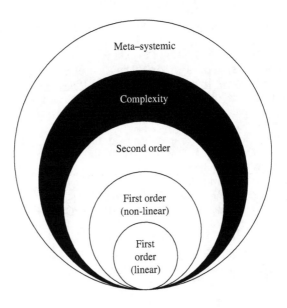

Theory in a nutshell

Chaos theory

Chaos theorists build mathematical models made up of inter-related non-linear equations. For certain parameter values, the whole system demonstrates stable, predictable patterns. At other values the system demonstrates highly unstable behaviour. Between these values, the system behaves in a way that looks random but in fact follows a pattern. Chaos in this sense is not random confusion. Chaos is an unnoticed pattern that we assume to be random.

In the 1960s a meteorologist called Edward Lorenz developed a model for weather forecasting. Weather patterns can be modelled in the form of non-linear equations representing temperature, pressure, humidity and wind speed. He ran a simulation and a particular weather pattern emerged. He ran it again and went for a coffee. When he returned he found that the outcome was completely different. He eventually tracked down the source of variation to having entered a piece of data to six decimal places the first time, and three decimal places the second time. A colleague, Phil Merilees, noted that if the results were representative, then one flap of a seagull's wings could change the course of the weather forever. A second colleague, Phil Mears, preferred butterflies, and came up with the title for a Lorenz paper 'Does the Flap of a Butterfly's Wings in Brazil Set Off a Tornado in Texas?' This was not to suggest it might be wise to hunt down and destroy every butterfly in Brazil. Rather, it was to frame the difficulty of making long-term weather predictions.

Though it is currently impossible to model the weather beyond a few days, the weather is not random. We don't get rainstorms in the desert, and it doesn't snow on Bondi Beach. The weather, whilst apparently random, does follow patterns. But these patterns don't repeat because small changes in the system have major impacts on system patterns. The weather forecaster may therefore get tomorrow's weather right but be hopeless at forecasting the weather three or four days out. Tiny local changes in temperature, pressure, humidity and wind speed can have an enormous impact on whole global weather systems. Hence, the seagull/butterfly effect.

Jurassic Park

In *Jurassic Park*, Jeff Goldblum plays the part of Dr Ian Malcolm. Dr Malcolm is out in a jeep one day with dinosaur experts Dr Alan Grant (Sam Neill) and Dr Ellie Satler (Laura Dern). While in the jeep, Dr Malcolm explains chaos theory.

Dr Malcolm: See, the tyrannosaur doesn't obey set patterns or park schedules. It's the essence of chaos.

Dr Satler: I'm still not clear on chaos.

Dr Malcolm: Oh, it simply deals with predictability in complex systems. The shorthand is the butterfly effect. The butterfly effect is when it flaps its wings in Peking and in Central Park you get rain instead of sunshine.

Dr Satler: (*Indicates she doesn't understand.*)

Dr Malcolm: (*Takes Ellie's hair in his hand for some reason.*) Am I going too fast? I go too fast. Give me that glass of water. We're going to do an experiment. It should be still. The car's bouncing up and down. But that's OK – it's just an example. Now put your hand flat like a hieroglyphic then . . . now let's say a drop of water falls on your hand. Which way's the drop going to roll off? (*Drops some water on her hand.*). Ah-ha! OK! Now freeze your hand, freeze your hand. Don't move. I'm going to do the same thing, start with the same place again. Which way's it going to roll off do you think?

Dr Satler: Let's say back. Same way.

Dr Malcolm: Back. Same place (*Drops more water on her hand and takes Ellie's hair in his hand again.*) Ha! It changed. Why? (*Takes her hand in his.*) Because tiny variations of the orientation of the hairs on your hand. (*Strokes her hand.*)

Dr Satler: Alan, look at this.

Dr Malcolm: The amount of blood that's in your vessels, imperfections in the skin.

Dr Satler: Imperfections in the skin?

Dr Malcolm: Microscopic, microscopic. They never repeat and vastly affect the outcome. That's the point.

Dr Satler:	Unpredictability.
Dr Grant:	(*Suddenly jumps out of the jeep.*)
Dr Malcolm:	There. Look at this. See, see? I'm right again. Nobody could have predicted that Dr Grant would suddenly jump out of a moving vehicle.
Dr Satler:	(*Takes her hand back and also jumps out of the jeep.*)
Dr Malcolm:	(*To himself.*) There's another example. See here I am now by myself, talking to myself. That's chaos theory.[1]

Whilst Dr Malcolm's rather creepy behaviour may quite *easily* explain why he finds himself alone in the jeep, this is nevertheless quite a good explanation of chaos theory, in that it makes clear that chaos is not randomness, nor is it a lack of order. When Ian Malcolm drops the water on Ellie Salter's hand, it doesn't evaporate. It doesn't shoot off sideways. It doesn't retreat back into the glass. First it goes one way, and then it goes another way, even though Ellie's hand is in the same place each time. Look closer, however, and there is a recurring pattern of activities including the movement of blood in her blood vessels, slight movements of the hair on her hands, and so on. What appears random is ordered, but the pattern is hidden. The behaviour of the water drop is both predictable (in that we have a pretty good idea of the various ways the drop could fall) and unpredictable (in that we have no idea how exactly it will fall). It is predictably unpredictable, or unpredictably predictable. Given the extent to which Dr Malcolm is playing uninvited with Dr Salter's hair and hands, her sudden departure from the vehicle is perhaps more predictable.

This is the essence of chaos theory. It is different to first order systems thinking, in that the relationship between variables is seen to be so complex that we cannot expect the world to behave predictably. It is different to second order systems thinking in that it posits that all system dynamics can ultimately be modelled and understood. In this sense, chaos theory is similar to both first and second order systems theories in that it encourages us to compare the behaviours of people in an organisation to the functioning of other systems and to seek out ways of predicting and controlling those behaviours.

Complex adaptive systems

Unlike all the systems so far described, a complex adaptive system (CAS) is capable of spontaneous change.[2] A CAS consists of multiple agents, and each of these agents behaves according to its own set of rules. These rules determine the response of an agent to the behaviour of other agents.

Craig Reynolds created a computer simulation called *Boids*.[3] A 'boid' in this case is a computer version of a bird. He was interested in understanding the flocking behaviour of migrating birds. How do they manage to fly in perfect formation? He required each of his computer boids to follow just three simple rules. For example, they had to maintain a minimum distance from other boids, and they had to fly at the same speed as other boids. Following these simple rules, his boids flew in perfect formation, like real flocks of birds. Reynolds therefore succeeded in demonstrating how single agents adhering to simple rules can result in an apparently complex overall pattern. His boids flew through the sky in perfect formation. This is interesting, but it may not help us much to understand the behaviour of people in organisations, because people in organisations don't all follow the same rules.

Thomas Ray conducted a more complex computer simulation that he called Tierra.[4] The first inhabitant of Tierra was a digital organism comprising 80 instructions on how to self-replicate. The creature's offspring were not identical to the original creature, and different types of creature evolved.

Among the first creatures to evolve were the parasites. Parasites were too short to replicate themselves, but they borrowed code from other agents and replicated anyway. Parasites replicated faster and faster until they became the dominant organism, at which point their capacity to borrow code from other organisms diminished. A different form of the original creature also evolved. These were the hyper-parasites, able to detect and avoid parasites. Starved of code, the parasites become extinct. Social hyper-parasites emerged, which replicated in unison with each other. Then cheaters appeared, who exploited the interaction between hyper-parasites to hijack code and use it for their own replication.

The simulation demonstrated the capacity of a system to self-organise, and again, how broad patterns emerge unplanned. The overall pattern that emerged in Tierra was a function of interactions between agents, each of which was following a set of rules. But knowledge of those rules doesn't enable a bystander to predict outcomes with confidence.

Micro / macro

If we think of an organisation as a complex adaptive system, it follows that I need to seek to understand what is happening at a micro (or local) level if I am to understand what is happening at the macro (or organisational) level. The overall pattern (macro) is a consequence of all of the activity taking place locally (micro).

For example, management launches a new set of values. These values require staff to do what they say they will do (integrity), to respect others (respect) and to get things done (achieve). Management has a vision of staff all collaborating with each other, making realistic commitments to each other, thereby achieving great things. Soon after the launch, folks in the Operations team refer to the new values in complaining to Marketing that onsite promotions are always delivered late. The Marketing team is unhappy with the way the Operations team speak to them, citing a lack of respect. Marketing and Operations both focus on making sure they achieve their goals without consulting with the other team. They both claim to be achieving, even though promotions overall are badly executed. Elsewhere, the IT team is spending lots of time in meetings, making sure that everyone's view is taken into account in the design of new systems (respect). As a consequence, system delivery is slowing down.

Six months later, something seems to have changed across the whole organisation. People are head-down making sure they complete their individual deliverables. Everyone is talking about respect and integrity, usually with reference to the failures of others. If one was to try to capture prevailing actual values, they would be something like autonomy, individual excellence, and complaining. If management were to try and work out why this happened, then they would have to examine in great detail how their messaging was received, who in each function of the organisation took the message and translated it, how people responded to the translation and interpreted it, and how different functions then interacted with each other based on the outcomes of local meaning-making. But senior management members don't usually do this because they are thinking through a first order lens. They can see no reason why the espoused values were not taken up. They become angry and frustrated with people further down the organisation for being obstructive, uncooperative and 'resistant to change'. Were they instead to become curious about what is happening at a local level, then they would begin to understand much better what they are experiencing on a broader level. And they could start thinking about how to participate more effectively in the myriad of conversations taking place across the organisation.

In and out of the system

First and second order systems thinking both enable us to regard the organisation as a system, from the outside. The outside agent, be it coach and coachee, or leader and team, sit and talk about the organisation as if it is a machine of some kind, working to a set of rules. The rules may be linear or non-linear, but the rules can be discerned or at least hypothesised. The outside observers work out what they need to do to change the system so that it delivers the desired outcome. Through the complexity lens the idea of stepping outside the system to plot an intervention makes no sense. The leader is part of the system, and her interactions with others, including trusted peers and her coach, represent micro activities within the system. The micro activities she is in engaged in happen alongside lots of other micro activities she may not even be aware of, that equally impact on the functioning of the system. She can't hope to step out of the system, take an action, and then step back into the system expecting to succeed in redirecting the system to achieve my desired outcomes. There is no stepping outside of the system.

Returning to the story about values, senior management might respond to the situation by introducing a new value called 'collaboration'. Through a complexity lens they would be better off acknowledging they have no control over events, that they are functioning as part of the system whether they like it or not and working out how they might play a more effective role in the system. Perhaps by venturing out into the organisation and engaging in dialogue.

Through a complexity lens, when a leader engages with her peers (and coach) to discuss the system, she recognises that she is following her own prescribed set of behaviours. She is engaged in conversation with others, who follow different guiding principles. From these interactions emerge new intention and actions. Elsewhere in the organisation,

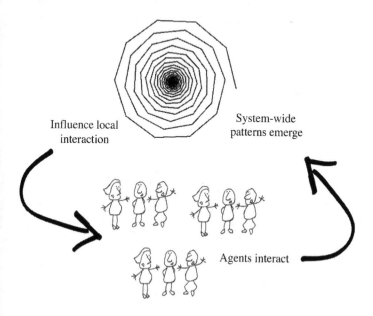

Figure 5.1 A Complex Adaptive System (CAS)

other people are interacting too, each person following their own unique behavioural profile. Other intentions and actions emerge. The coming together of multiple intentions and actions results in a new and unpredictable overall pattern of behaviours. Through this complexity lens the leader cannot hope to *direct* the energies of an organisation, either on her own or in collaboration with a select few. This does not mean, however, that she is helpless (like Evan and Frank in the movies). She gets to influence. Indeed, she influences through every interaction she engages in, wittingly or unwittingly. She just doesn't get to control.

Strange attractors

The idea here is that a complex adaptive system can flip from one pattern to another as it is pulled from one 'strange attractor' to another.[5] I was privy to a good example of this phenomenon during COVID-19. I was allowed to listen to a conversation between senior executives at a large financial services firm during the early stages of lockdown. This was an organisation that had been making huge efforts over a number of years to get people in different divisions of the organisation to collaborate more. The divisions tended to focus exclusively on the needs of their clients and to replicate functions that existed in other division – digital solutions, for example. The pull to satisfy immediate client needs had the system stuck in a particular pattern that resisted all purposeful efforts to shift it. Then one day, a few weeks into the COVID-19 pandemic, some of the senior executives noticed that divisions had suddenly started working together. Client needs had shifted and continued to change almost on a daily basis. Client facing executives in each of the divisions adapted quickly, working out how best to satisfy these merging needs. They reached out, without hesitation, to other colleagues in other divisions to work on these new needs. The old pattern wasn't functioning. It had been pushed to its limit by a new set of circumstances, and so it flipped into a new pattern without anyone directing it to do so. The senior executives were very pleased and vowed to make sure people didn't slip back into old behaviours, but they may be disappointed. If the pull of the old strange attractor is felt again, patterns of behaviour may flip back, without anyone understanding why.

Philosophy

Looking through the complexity lens a coach is likely to share some or all of the following perspectives:

1 Perspective on system

Consistent with the previous ways of thinking, the organisation is still a system, with sub-systems and boundaries, but the system operates to different rules than do the systems envisaged before. This system cannot be directed or controlled. It is a system in which big patterns are a consequence of smaller, local patterns. And smaller local patterns are impacted by bigger, more macro patterns. As an advocate of the first order philosophies, the coach believes the system is hardwired and she looks for the rules that determine how the system operates. The second order coach also believes in hardwiring, but not in Man's capacity to directly discern the nature of that hardwiring.

Through a complexity lens the system is not hard-wired at all. What happens in the system is a consequence of local interaction and the coming together of different patterns of micro patterns. So, the coach needs to look micro and macro to have any chance of understanding what's happening. In the case of the COVID-19 example, cited earlier, the coach is attuned to noticing shifts of behaviour at the macro level and hypothesising what might be pushing the system to a place where macro patterns change. At the same time, she is interested in understanding what is happening at the micro level in different parts of the organisation.

For example, the CEO of BigBank plc announces a 10% reduction in salary across the board to reflect a sudden decline in profits. The complexity coach notices an overall shift in behaviour across the BigBank. A gulf appears between the senior executive layer and layers below. At the same time, people in the lower levels spend more time talking together, not only within their functions, but across functions. The system has adopted a new pattern. The coach notices how the macro pattern seems to have flipped in response to a new 'strange attractor'.

The coach is also keen to understand the micro. She heads out into the organisation to understand what sense people are making of the announcement. In one team, in one geographic office, people are fixed on the salaries of senior staff relative to less senior staff. Why don't senior staff bear the brunt of the pain, since they made the decisions that led to the problem, and since they can most afford it? In another part of the organisation, people understand the need to cut costs but, because they are very busy, wonder why staff in less busy parts of the bank are not simply being made redundant. One division, that has been looking to become autonomous for a while, makes a case for their piece of the business to be spun off and sold; sales revenues could buffer the rest of the organisation through the current period of hardship. In each locality, various perspectives come together, and collective viewpoints emerge. These collective viewpoints merge and from that mergence comes another, broader narrative. The complexity coach is interested in helping BigBank's leadership better understand what is happening in this complex system, so they feel confident deciding how to best further engage.

2 Perspective on people

The complexity perspective recognises an important flaw in second order thinking. Second order thinking says we are all frogs, with a highly personal interpretation of events. The second order perspective encourages us to build a hypothetical version of reality leveraging the perceptions of lots of frogs (a *knot* of frogs). But a frog is a frog. Whilst each frog may see things differently, no frogs see things that move. To elicit the views of many frogs may yield a collective perspective that isn't much more insightful than the perspective of the single frog.

The complexity perspective says don't worry about getting a load of frogs to exit the system to talk about what's going on. You *can't* exit the system. The leader cannot exit the system. Conversations between coach and leader, or coach and executive team, are just examples of conversations happening inside the system. There are many other local conversations happening across the system at the same time, and each plays a role in the emergence of new meaning and behaviour. No one gets to step outside. The coach therefore is as active an agent in these local conversations as anyone else. The coach is no more and no less neutral than anyone else in the system. Everything the coach says (or doesn't say) or implies through body language, impacts on outcomes. Every choice the coach makes is impactful and is different to the choice that the coach-next-door would make. The coach is as much an active co-creator of change as is anyone else in, or associated with, the organisation.

The idea that positional power is sacrosanct is lost too. The great leader cannot stand outside the system to make changes to the system that will be acted upon by compliant parts. The leader can influence. She can travel the system to engage in conversation with people in different parts of the system, and what she says and does *will* influence what happens next. But what happens next is still only unpredictably predictable.

3 Perspective on change

If the world is volatile, complex and ambiguous, then of course outcomes are unpredictable. No one can predict what happens when a group of people engage in conversation. Some coaches get upset when their coachees:

- Take too long to come up with goals
- Don't follow through on actions they've committed to
- Decide they don't want any more coaching
- Are hard to contact for long periods

These events are contrary to some traditional coaching beliefs. For example:

- Coachees need to come up with goals early on in an assignment. If they don't, then they're not committed, or the coach isn't doing a good job.
- Every coaching session ends with actions (otherwise it's just a conversation, etc.).

- A committed coachee does what they say they will do.
- If the coachee is hard to contact, or says they don't want any more coaching, it's because the coach isn't doing a good job.

The complexity coach recognises these mantras and recognises that they have emerged from conversations between coaches, coach educators and clients. These mantras are based on the way the world 'should' be and an underlying first order philosophy that attributes a specific cause to every outcome. The complexity coach is determinedly unsurprised by any of the aforementioned events and curious as to their significance. If a coachee is hard to contact, it could mean any of a number of things. For example:

- Something new came up and the coachee reprioritised their time
- Something new came up and the coachee felt over-whelmed
- The coachee wanted to spend more time considering an insight that came up in the previous session
- The coachee is still experimenting with a new behaviour
- The coachee tried out a new behaviour and it didn't work, and is embarrassed to recount the story to you
- The coachee's line manager mocked him for working with a coach
- The coachee's partner is unwell
- The coachee got fired and no one told you (this happened to me once)

Given the extent to which all of our intentions evolve, through the changing of circumstance and the sense we make of change through our conversations with others, of course we cannot predict what will happen next. Our coachees are not autonomous individuals who reflect only with us. They are social creatures whose perspectives on life are constantly changing through their interaction with others. When things don't go as planned, this is data – something to be explored and to learn from. Not something to get grumpy about.

Coaches looking at the world through a complexity lens are comfortable with conflict and potential conflict. They are comfortable asking coachees why they cancelled sessions. They are comfortable probing deeper into why coachees didn't follow through on commitments. They are comfortable being rapped on the knuckles by clients unhappy with something they did. Everyone looks at the world differently. In any given scenario, multiple people are interpreting events differently. Change happens in an organisation, not when the leader of that organisation decrees it, but when people with different perspectives voice those different opinions. When someone contradicts me, I have a choice. I can refer to my universal truth and seek to win an argument, or I can explore the other person's perspective. Criticism tells us as much about the critic as it does about the person being criticised. To understand how change is happening in an organisation, I need to regard that organisation as a pattern of perspectives, all in relationship to each other.

The task of the leader is to explore the pattern of perspectives and to engage in those relationships. This is how a leader gets to influence change. And the leader does have a powerful voice. Whilst it is correct to suggest that first and second order perspectives over-privilege positional power, positional power is still relevant. The leader just needs to remember that other forms of power exist as well. This is how the coach thinks about change through a complexity lens.

4 Perspective on power

In organisational life today, the idea that leaders control outcomes still pervades. Even through a first order lens, it is recognised that old 'command and control' strategies don't work, because people (unlike cogs in a machine) need to be motivated if they are to do their best. So, today's leaders don't just tell people what to do, they seek to motivate the person to whom they are giving the order. Nevertheless, the role of the leader remains to get things done. To fail in this regard is to fail as a leader. Whilst the second order perspective acknowledges the fallibility of individual perception, including the perception of the leader, the leader is still held accountable for getting things done. Positional power is still sacrosanct. The enlightened second order leader knows not to try to lead an organisation solely through force of will. Leadership is a collaborative exercise, but still individual accountability is there to be respected and exercised.

The complexity coach thinks differently. The complexity coach doesn't discount the idea that positional power exists and can occasionally directly yield desired outcomes. But when it comes to leading wide-scale change in a complex world, the coach recognises the limitations of positional power. To assert that change cannot be controlled is not to be fatalist. Wide-scale change across big organisations cannot be directed or controlled, but it can be influenced. We are not saying that change will run its own course, no matter what. We are saying that change emerges from the interaction between local agent and that power has a role to play. The leader, or indeed anyone else in an organisation, not only can but does influence change.

The emergence of change often goes unnoticed. We may mistakenly attribute it to individual brilliance. Consider the CEO faced with a crucial decision – should I go ahead and acquire a competitor or not? On the way to work he stops for a coffee. The barista winks at him as she hands over his coffee and says, 'Be lucky!'. The CEO squares his shoulders and decides to be brave. He approves the acquisition and it turns out to be a brilliant decision. The barista's contribution goes unrecognised. The complexity worldview is one in which every utterance has the potential for impacting others. We don't control the impact of our utterances, so we don't know the extent to which what we say influences others, or how. But we can hypothesise.

In hypothesising how change is happening, we must consider power. But we need to look beyond positional power. There are many forms of power, and different people are differentially subject to each of these forms of power. Positional power isn't of much use when trying to persuade someone to do something when they are hoping to be made redundant. Positional power isn't of much use if the person I am talking to knows that no one will know whether he has made an effort to comply or not. Positional power isn't of much use if the people I am attempting to command have better relationships than I do with the people above me. I may have positional power, but my influence on events may still be relatively weak when compared to people with more relationship power, network power, expert power, etc. This perspective shifts our focus gently away from individual agency, and the attributes and personalities of individuals, to the relationships between people.

For example, Sally is the CEO, and she thinks the organisation needs to pay more attention to customers. She could attempt to impose this view on the organisation, implementing new systems and reviewing reward and recognition schemes to ensure desired behaviours. The extent to which she is successful will determine the extent to which she thinks she will be seen as a great leader. She works hard to refine her message, to make the argument and to make sure people comply with new expectations. On her travels she sees a few people doing a great job and calls attention to their efforts. Sally works hard, taking the message around different offices and monitoring people's behaviours. She gets tired and becomes discouraged when told that not everyone is compliant. The new system has been installed, but not everyone is using it properly. Sally begins to feel like the little boy trying to plug every new hole appearing in the wall of the dyke. Change happens anyway. Customer-facing staff start giving away bigger discounts because customers don't like the new service offering. Call centre staff stop trying to solve issues themselves and pass issues on to specialists to resolve. The systems budget blows out such that other systems enhancements can't be implemented. Change happens, but it isn't the change Sally wanted. Sally begins to doubt her 'leadership', her capacity to diagnose an issue, come up with a solution and align everyone around her way of thinking. The problem here, through a complexity lens, is that Sally has misunderstood what leadership is.

Through a complexity lens, Sally recognises that 'leadership' is a collective activity. She picks key audiences with whom to share her views and who she feels she needs to listen to. This includes not only her leadership team but also a diverse mix of others across the organisation, including lots of people who spend their day talking to clients, and who design and implement systems. Throughout these interactions she disciplines herself to listen without prejudice, to do her best to see things through others' eyes. As she does so, she notices her perspective evolving. She senses that the systems team is used to pointing out risks and used to being ignored. She calls a meeting to talk to them only about risk. Customer service staff invite her to listen into calls. She comes to understand some of the issues that most frustrate certain customer segments. She gives people more space to make decisions, at the same time holding people more accountable for high-level outcomes. Three months later she reads the latest system specification and is delighted with how innovative it appears to be. The designers have wound back on the system's functionality, putting more faith in individual decision making on the part of the operator. She reflects on what happened and celebrates how something special seems to have emerged from the collective. It's hard to know who contributed what, but she has an intuitive sense that the new approach will lead to great outcomes.

5 Perspective on team coaching

From a complexity perspective, team coaching looks different. Some team coaching theorists suggest we pay most attention to helping people clarify roles, objectives and individual accountabilities. If you succeed in clarifying these aspects of team, then the team will be more impactful and the team will be happy. There is no need to talk about team dynamics. Talking about the relationship between team members in itself may be enjoyable but has no impact on team performance. This feels very much like a first or second order perspective, in which the team is an agent of change that can of itself make change happen. There is no need to explore the relational nature of change if coach, team leader and team believe they can stand outside the system (the rest of the organisation), plot an intervention and execute it. If that is how change works, then all they need to do is make sure the team pulls the right levers. Sometimes, of course, this approach works. And when it doesn't work, we can blame the intransigence of others.

Through a complexity lens, the coach is interested in how the team comes up with its intentions. If the coach can help the team become aware of how it comes up with its intentions, then the team will get better at working through complex problems. As the team develops its capacity to understand and manage its own interpersonal dynamics, so it will get better at engaging with people outside the team and improve its capacity to influence change. It will no longer blame others for their intransigence if the team is unsuccessful. Instead, it will consider its own capacity to navigate that apparent intransigence.

Purpose

A coach thinking through this lens is bound to pay attention to patterns of behaviour and power across the system. Every conversation happening in the organisation has potential significance. The notion of the autonomous individual ceases to make complete sense, and so the coach may be more likely to couch their purpose in terms of their potential impact on the wider system, or the organisation. Being asked to make a choice between individual and organisational needs, should individual and organisation disagree as to the focus for coaching, makes less sense. Everyone's needs are intertwined.

Practice

Kelly and Allen

Kelly and Allen again meet to discuss the sudden increase in sales. Allen is bemused. Kelly tells Allen about chaos theory and shows him the clip from *Jurassic Park*.

Allen: So, what do I tell the executive team if our sales suddenly go up or down? That a seagull flapped its wings in Bournemouth?

Kelly: If your executive team is like anyone else's executive team, then don't expect an easy ride. We all like to think we are in control of events. But the seagull story illustrates the fallacy of believing that we always understand events, let alone control them. But your executive team knows that already. They know we can't forecast the weather, exchange rates, stock prices . . .

Allen: Train timetables . . .

Kelly: Exactly.

Allen: I need more than the seagull story.

Kelly: Of course. What else do you need?

Allen: Well, if you're saying that chaos isn't the same as randomness, that there is an underlying pattern behind events, then it says we should keep trying to understand what happened in July. That we might not be looking for something big, that it might have been something really quite minor that triggered something more significant, and that whatever happened may have happened earlier than July.

Kelly: What else?

Allen: Well, that we need to understand that we might never work out what that small thing was, such that we never work out exactly what happened. In which case we have to assume something similar might happen again, perhaps for different reasons. That the nature of the market may be changing in ways we don't understand, and we have to change the way we think about things like inventory management. We need to be more adaptive.

Kelly: How does that feel as a story?

Allen: Uncomfortable. But I think it's context at least. There's a story in there somewhere about complexity and a need to look at things differently, and a need to change the way we think about things. With a bit more work, a *lot* more work, I think we can integrate these ideas into the way we operate and help the executive team understand that we do know what we're doing, and that we're doing a good job. But we need a theory as to what's happened, and a theory as to what might happen next and how we can effectively intervene.

Kelly: What do you think might be happening?

Allen: I suspect the answer lies in what's happening in the online communities again. We used to get focus groups together to talk about our business and extract learnings. With social media it's like focus groups are constantly forming and reforming, always talking. And we don't get to choose who participates or to set rules as to how we want people to interact. We still need to get better at working with these virtual communities. We've done some work since last we spoke. Some people keep talking about trying to *manage* these online exchanges. Putting out messages to tell people what to think. Others talk about setting up official forums. Given what we've just talked about I think they may be missing the point. They may be still thinking in terms of control – be it your first or second order paradigms. We need to get out there and just watch what's going on. We need to engage in some of these forums ourselves and just be present and curious. We need to listen, then get in there and participate and just see what happens.

Reflecting on the conversation, Kelly felt uneasy; the idea that no one can control or predict events. Many of her clients would not accept that. At the same time she thought of things happening in her life that she couldn't explain. In one way, thinking about complexity felt like taking off a heavy jacket. If the world was this complex, then she couldn't possibly be expected to have the answer for everything. But some of her coachees would continue to be frustrated by this fundamental challenge to their way of looking at the world, the idea that logical rational thought would always help you get to the bottom of things. That leaders could control outcomes all the time. She came across a model in a book that characterised different scenarios, the Stacey Matrix (Figure 5.2).[6]

The Stacey matrix suggests we can diagnose when things are simple, when they are complicated and when they are complex. I can then adjust my thinking and approach to the situation. If the situation is simple, I can safely assume a first order approach will do the job. When the situation is complicated, I may need to think through a non-linear lens. Kelly need only worry about the complexity perspective with Allen because of the kinds of challenges he is facing. With other coachees, she can happily continue to use first and second order approaches. This complexity stuff is a whole different domain and requires a shift in thinking for her and Allen. Still an uncomfortable thought, but at least she now felt she had a compass.

Next session

Another session, another issue. This time Allen is angry. He is angry that he and the team are finding it hard to engage people with the new strategy. After getting the plan signed

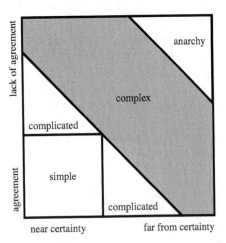

Figure 5.2   Stacey Matrix

off by the executive team, he and the team spent several hours together with the HR and Communications Director, crafting a super-clear message to explain the new strategy and what its implementation would entail. He and the rest of the team then went out to the organisation with great enthusiasm, to align everyone toward the new vision. Allen himself conducted two Town Hall presentations to the whole sales and marketing team. The problem was, no one was doing what they were supposed to do.

Allen: For example, I went to a meeting of all the regional store managers. I explained how we were going to coordinate social media campaigns with in-store campaigns and use in-store campaign materials to direct people to our online website. Some of them understood it, but others said it would just result in lower store sales.

Kelly: It will, won't it?

Allen: We don't think so. Our planning scenarios suggest that people who want to shop online will shop online, regardless of the brand.

Kelly: Then why advertise to them in-store if they shop online?

Allen: You sound like one of the regional managers! Because it's about now that people are shifting their behaviours. Some of the people visiting our stores may be visiting for the last time, or if not the last time we're still not going to see them around as much. So, we need to make it easy for them to find us online and persuade them by means of a good offer. Right now, we have a 30% discount on offer in the online shop that we don't have in store.

Kelly: I bet the store managers are getting complaints about that!

Allen: Again, you sound like one of them. We've modelled all this, and the analysis clearly shows that this strategy leads to the best outcome for the business as a whole. It's so clear – it does not matter what scenarios you run; the results always support the strategy. We've run it 100 times. The whole of the team believes it, we all know it's true. We've proved it to ourselves and shared the evidence with everyone in the organisation.

Kelly: You said the whole team supports the strategy?

Allen: Pretty much, yes. It's so frustrating. You read about this in books, but I never thought it would happen to me.

Kelly: Never thought what would happen to you?

Allen: This 'resistance to change' stuff. Middle management just sitting on their hands saying it doesn't make sense when it clearly does make sense. It can only be inertia, a reluctance to put in an extra bit of effort. Perhaps even a bit of stupidity. I think we've got some capability issues further down the chain. Not sure how we let that happen!

Kelly: What about other teams? Don't you need support from finance and IT to make this happen?

Allen: Sure, we do. We'll need more capacity online and finance needs to help us run the scenarios, to make sure we get the numbers right. And they need to be right behind the discounting scheme, but they know it's just a one-off, very strategic.

Kelly: So, they are all behind you?

Allen: We're getting there. We've had some problems with the reliability of the product ordering system, and there does seem to be a lack of urgency in addressing those issues, but I reckon those are just teething problems.

Kelly: Hmmm. Are you not reminded of chaos theory?

Allen: What do you mean?

Kelly: One unhappy customer starts making noises online . . . In this case sounds like you have a few of your team making noises.

Allen: We will get it sorted out. And Finance will be with us too, once we get them over the line on the discounting scheme.

Kelly: They're not behind it now?

Allen: Officially they are.

Kelly: What's their objection?

Allen: They think the discount is too big, but we've proved the numbers work using their models. They've even run the models. So, it doesn't make sense. Their argument is illogical, wrong, and they'll have to come along on the journey.

Kelly: So basically, you have a *lot* of people who aren't convinced by your new strategy.

Allen: Some, but we've modelled it all, and we know how the organisation works and who needs to be onside. The executive team will make sure everyone does what they need to.

Kelly: You don't look so sure.

Allen: (*Grimaces.*) I'm not, but what else can we do? We've thought about this all systemically, we know how it needs to work and done our relationship mapping. What else is there?

Kelly: Well, I haven't met anyone from your systems team. But let's suppose that, over time, there has emerged a truth for that team, which is that if everyone is to have a work-life balance, and if their work is to be efficient, then new systems must be implemented progressively, according to a pre-agreed plan. I'm not talking about one person's beliefs, I'm talking about an orthodoxy that has emerged over time between these people, a mantra that determines how they respond to any request from the business.

Allen: That's no good if it stops us moving fast.

Kelly: That's *your* orthodoxy. To hit your numbers, you must have good customer intelligence, and the competition is forever coming up with new technological solutions for gathering client feedback faster. Whether or not the implementation of such systems was in last year's plan doesn't matter. Sales will tail off if the company doesn't adopt these new systems quickly. Speed matters more than planning a system down to the nth detail before taking action. I get it. But we can predict what will happen when you sit down and have a conversation with the Head of IT. . . .

Allen: Go on then, predict.

Kelly: Well, there are multiple scenarios here, of course. When I say we can predict what will happen I don't say we can predict what *will* happen. We can only hypothesise what *might* happen . . .

Allen: What *might* happen?

Kelly: OK. Well you and the Head of IT exchange views. From that conversation emerges a new plan of action, that the invention of a new customer intelligence system is outsourced and paid for by a special budget that you need to provide. The IT team will make sure the new solution meets the requirement of existing systems, and everyone will be happy. The Finance team now gets involved. They believe in financial discipline and present you with a standard template to use in making a business case for the new technological system. The problem is that it's the IT department who will need to fill out much of the form because they will need to check out the outsourced suppliers' specifications and ensure that the new solution can be implemented through the current IT architecture. The IT team becomes cranky because they don't have time to conduct such an exercise and complain to HR. HR talks to you and IT, who agree to use a different supplier, used to working with the organisation, who can write that part of the proposal. The only issue is that their solution isn't as good as the original solution you had in mind. The CEO gets wind of what's going on and insists that the new solution be made available within three months. He's recently been to a workshop on the 'Fourth Industrial Revolution' where the case was made strongly that organisations must be adaptive and nimble. You and IT are held accountable for putting the new feedback process in face within 90 days, which you do. The CEO wakes up in three months' time and reads in the paper that the analysts are very unimpressed that his company has implemented a second-rate system. Why did it happen? The CEO is at a loss to provide a logical answer.

Allen: I hope that's not what happens.

Kelly: It's one of a hundred possible scenarios. Which one happens depends on the flapping of the butterfly's wings.

Allen: What can I do?

Kelly: Try flapping your wings. What *can* you do?

Allen: I need to get out into the organisation, is what you're saying. I need to understand how all these different groups of people are making sense of our strategy.

Kelly: You do seem very invested in the scenarios that you and team came up with, the calculations that said your strategy will work. I'm wondering how open you are to other perspectives.

Allen: The strategy is right; the numbers prove it.

Kelly: I know nothing about your business, but I do know how spreadsheets work. Your numbers prove your strategy is right if the assumptions you have fed into your model are right. I'm not saying they're wrong, but think back to the conversation we had about your planning cycle. You said you didn't want to build a plan based on new assumptions, and that you wanted to understand what different assumptions different members of your team might be making.

Allen: And the seagull story.

Kelly: What occurs to you?

Allen: If we're going to get out into the organisation and ask questions, then we need to be genuinely interested. If we go out there just looking to prove ourselves right, then it won't be a useful exercise. At the same time, we will have to be choiceful. We don't want to end up with the equivalent of a second-best client feedback system.

When Kelly returned, a few weeks later, Allen looked a lot happier. He and the team had, by and large, succeeded in engaging with others with an open mind. He had lost his temper once, with someone who told him the strategy was 'fanciful and deluded', but he quickly recovered his composure and succeeded in eliciting where that perspective was coming from. Kelly felt a warm feeling inside when Allen pointed a finger at her and told her that 'resistance to change' was just a misnomer for 'need to ask questions'. Having spoken widely across the organisation Allen and his team discovered that:

- Store managers were worried that the new strategy would result from job losses in the stores.
- The regional managers hadn't well understood the rationale of the new strategy. They were most preoccupied with the questions they were being asked by store managers and were listening mostly for what would happen to store staff. The rest of the message was getting lost.
- Two members of his own team were unconvinced. They worried that in-store advertising might encourage customers to explore multiple online stores, and that some of the assumptions built into the planning model might be wrong.
- Some of the staff in IT were friends with some of the in-store staff and didn't feel motivated to sort out reliability issues in the product ordering system.
- The Finance Director believed a 15% discount would serve just as well as a 30% discount. The Pricing Manager had attempted to persuade him to the contrary but

hadn't done a good job. The Finance Director had shared his concerns with the rest of his team.

As a consequence, Allen and the team spoke to the regional managers and explained that stores played an important role in their strategy for at least the next three to five years. Four stores were already operating at borderline profitability and were candidates for closure. Shoozon would look to redeploy those staff in stores where possible, and outplacement packages would be offered to others. The team also paid more careful attention to some of the assumptions in the model and identified a couple of assumptions that would need early testing. A pilot scheme was set up in one particular region to test those assumptions. More people were on board than before, and though still not everyone was aligned, the team had a better idea how to go about responding to that discordance.

As she walked out to the carpark, Kelly felt the whole system surrounding her. She recognised she was as much a part of the system as Allen and his team were. That every word she spoke, as well as every word that Allen spoke, had an impact on the system. To be systemic she reflected, meant to be at ease with uncertainty, to be committed to engaging directly with others in the system, open to the emergence of new outcomes. First and second order ways of thinking now wore a 'handle-with-care' badge. They may prove useful in some scenarios, but you had to be careful not to hold on too carefully to any vision of the 'truth' and you had to be aware that not only the coachee, but you, too, were a part of the whole system, and that you as an agent in that system had only a limited perspective of the whole. She started to wonder about the Stacey Matrix and if it was really useful. How could you think like this only some of the time and not all the time?

A month later

As Kelly left for work, her two young children were arguing. Stevie, the ten-year-old, was mimicking his mother and telling Katie, the seven-year-old, to clean away her breakfast dishes. Stevie was doing a good job of imitating her, she thought, walking with a straight back and talking in a low, calm voice.

He pointed at Katie's cereal bowl and said, "Put it in the dishwasher please, Katie." Katie scowled, folded her arms and made no move to comply.

"She's not doing it, mum," Stevie complained. "How can I help if she won't do as I say? I'm older than her. She *should* do what I say."

"You're not the boss of me," said Katie, glowering. "No one is. I do what I like."

"Thank you for the thought, Stevie," said Kelly, putting her coat on. "Perhaps let me worry about what Katie does, but I do appreciate the effort. Now in the car please, both of you."

Now it was Stevie's turn to look cross. He grabbed his jacket and walked slowly to the car.

Kelly dropped the kids off at school and went to Allen's office. Allen had asked Kelly to sit in with his team for a session. Some team members were engaging enthusiastically with the organisation in working out how to move forward at any given point in time, others were not. Two members were particularly unhappy. Allen asked Kelly to facilitate a group coaching session, where members of the team could compare experiences and learn from each other. The session started out well enough, with Helen recounting with enthusiasm how she was engaging effectively with some of her regional managers. She was meeting with them once a fortnight for a couple of hours to hear how the new campaign was going and to create a space for everyone to share their experiences and concerns. As a consequence, certain aspects of the campaign had been tweaked in some of the regions, to accommodate the needs and wants of the store managers. Results were going well, with sales up 15% year-on-year. Some of the team nodded appreciatively. Simon didn't. Simon was in Helen's team. He looked after store promotions.

Simon: I don't understand why you're spending so much time encouraging them to push back on what we've sent out. It means my staff having to stay back late and do reworks. Just tell them what they're supposed to do and hold them to account.

Helen: I do hold them to account Simon, but I listen to them first. Much of what they say makes sense. If, ultimately, I don't agree, then we don't do it, but I make the time to listen first.

Simon: It doesn't make sense to me. It just slows things down and creates work.

Allen: What would happen if you did as Simon suggested, Helen?

Helen: (*Shrugs.*) They'd do as they were told. It might not be perfectly executed, because in their heart of hearts they wouldn't believe in it, and they'd prioritise other things, but they'd do it. Problem is, results wouldn't be as good, and I'd end up with twice as much work.

Simon: You'd have less work because everything would be more efficient.

Helen: I'd have more work, Simon, because results wouldn't be as good, and I'd be under pressure from Allen to improve sales. And my staff wouldn't come up with any ideas as to how we might improve sales, because I would have demonstrated that I wasn't interested in what they have to say. So, the onus would all be on me to improve sales in each and every store, when I don't know the customers in each and every store. And all my best store managers would eventually leave to work for other organisations who listen to their store managers.

Simon: It's not the store manager's job to come up with new ideas. That's our job. Their job is to get things done quickly and efficiently. You come up with the plan at the beginning of the year, implement, review, implement.

Helen: At the beginning of the year we said we were going to spend $3 million refitting stores. Given where we've got to now, that would have been a waste of money.

Simon: We didn't need the store managers to tell us that. We worked it out for ourselves and came up with the new campaign.

Helen: A campaign which we have subsequently tailored to individual stores with a subsequent increase in sales of about 5%, I believe.

Simon: How do you come up with 5%? You can't be sure.

Helen: No, I can't be sure. But I do know that my best performing store is located in an area with a high Mandarin-speaking population, and my second highest performing store is in an area with a high population of second-generation migrants from Vietnam. In both cases they helped us rewrite the copy in Mandarin/Vietnamese. The original translations were clunky and hard to understand, apparently. And both store managers have built up great local networks, spreading the word without anyone telling them to.

Simon: Just because they *said* the original translations were clunky and hard to understand . . .

Helen: I sought out second and third opinions, Simon. The fact is that we will never understand the changing needs of all of our customers without seeking the opinion of those who enjoy a different perspective than we do. Our customer base is too diverse. It's about leveraging different perspectives. Surely we learned that through the whole strategy planning exercise. Initially we ignored the views of Store Managers and IT and Finance, and had we not started listening, I can assure you I wouldn't be reporting 15% sales increases.

Kelly: Simon, you clearly have a different view?

Simon: I do. There's nothing wrong with collecting data to make decisions. You need to collect data. The data helps you make the right decisions.

Kelly: What about Helen's point, that those two store managers took your in-store materials and by tweaking them, came up with even more effective campaigns?

Simon: That may be so, but had they just gone ahead and done as they were told, I don't think we would have sold a lot less shoes, but we would have paid a lot less overtime.

Allen: I guess we'll never know for sure, but I think there's a bigger issue at play here. You may argue that in this case we would have made more money by incurring less cost. I think that's around the detail of that particular decision. What I think less contentious is that our business has become more complex, and that if we want to make good decisions we have to elicit the perspectives of people from across the organisation and be genuinely interested in what they have to say. Think about how we did planning last year.

Helen: Horrendous.

Simon: I admit, not good. We were asked to increase sales 5% in a declining market with no investment funds. But that's because the executive team misunderstood the data. They failed to recognise the impact of two new competitors into the market.

Helen: Why did they misunderstand the data when everyone in sales and marketing knew perfectly well what the impact would be?

Simon: They didn't listen.

Helen: They didn't ask. They just assumed they knew best, and they assumed it was their role to know best. That's still how we operate sometimes. Remember that stuff on first and second order thinking that Allen shared with us a few months ago? The executive team still sits down by itself to come up with an overall strategy for the business. Then we get to hear what we are expected to deliver and we are held to account to those objectives for the rest of the year even if they don't make any sense.

Remember the fuss everyone made when our sales went up 20% and no one could explain why. These guys have a fixation with being in control, and so do we. Once the plan is agreed, our job is to deliver. Never mind what may be happening in the market, the onus is on delivering the numbers, no matter what. So, people stop talking and we all stop learning.

Simon: It's still not an efficient way to operate.

Helen: Perhaps it's not an either/or. If we shift our thinking, recognising the need to be adaptive and flexible, perhaps we can find a way of doing things that is more efficient than the way we do things now.

Simon: It's a thought.

Helen: What's the thought?

Simon: First, I want to know what Kelly is thinking.

Kelly: I think you guys seem comfortable expressing different views, and you seem to be open to listening to each other. That's important.

Simon: Why? Seems to me we spend too much time talking to each other instead of getting out there and making stuff happen.

Kelly: I worked once for a company whose CEO said that he expected leaders to neither under-deliver nor over-deliver against their numbers. He didn't want them to under-deliver for obvious reasons. He didn't want to over-deliver either, because this implied people had set easy plans for themselves. The implication was that if we think long and hard enough about what is possible at the beginning of the planning cycle, then we will come up with a plan that is neither too easy nor too hard to deliver. The flaw in this thinking is that things change. The 'neither too much nor too little' mantra implies that all changes are foreseeable and/ or that leaders can respond to such changes to achieve the same results, perhaps by force of will.

That organisation subsequently reported a long sequence of financial, safety and environmental disasters.

Simon: They didn't have good planning systems.

Kelly: I agree. They placed too much credence in the data they had access to. Their data was useful, but it was incomplete, and it quickly became outdated as the environment in which they operated shifted and changed.

Simon: (*Nods thoughtfully.*)

Kelly: The other thing I'd like to just highlight is this debate around who knows best. The central planning team or the staff on the ground. I'm not sure that a binary view is helpful.

Allen: Because every perspective is useful.

Kelly: Yes, that, and also the idea that we can determine anyway whose view is right. Your world is complex and fast moving. You'll never know for sure who is right and who is wrong. More important that you come up with a collective perspective enriched by as many perspectives as possible . . . (*looks at Simon*) . . . recognising that you can't spend days and weeks making every decision.

Allen: And if we are truly listening to others in that process, then we have to be open to the idea that the emerging narrative may deviate from the story we originally shared with the organisation.

Helen: And be comfortable with that. I'd like to know what Simon is thinking.

Simon: OK, but what am I then responsible for? What are you responsible for? Our Board expects us to articulate a long-term strategy and make sure it is implemented. Each of us has to be accountable for our part in implementing the plan. The leader has to have a vision and if the leader doesn't stick to the vision, he or she will be seen as wishy-washy.

Allen: We have to engage with the Board over time. Understand what their immediate concerns are and be seen to be addressing those concerns. And we must have a vision, as you say. But we know the vision evolves as our understanding of our business evolves. We have to help the Board see that too. Over time.

Afterwards

Kelly asks Allen what sense he made of the exchange between Helen and Simon.

Allen: Simon is frustrated. He believes in the leader-as-hero model. He thinks people should do as they are told and he believes in hierarchy. He can be quite tiring. He expects me to tell him what to do all the time.

Kelly: He likes data.

Allen: He does like data and doesn't respond well to people challenging the adequacy of his data.

Kelly: For example?

Allen: He presented a whole lot of data to my team, suggesting that the latest marketing campaign can't have worked because customer engagement scores didn't shift. Helen pointed out that HappyFeet lowered their prices just before the campaign started and suggested that the campaign must have had a big impact, otherwise engagement scores would have declined.

Kelly: What else occurs to you thinking through events from a complexity perspective?

Allen: We were naive to think that the organisation would embrace the new strategy immediately, without question. We should have spent a whole lot more time talking to people across the business understanding their perspective on how we're doing. We should be doing that as a matter of course, not waiting for when we have something to sell.

Katy: To sell?

Allen: That's what we did. We went out there like a half-assed sales force trying to sell a new washing powder. It's embarrassing when I think about it. We need to get a whole lot smarter about how we go about engaging people.

Kelly: What if they don't like the strategy?

Allen: Life isn't black and white. Different people will support different aspects of the plan and disagree with other aspects. That's OK and is to be expected. First, we need to understand. Then we need to regroup and adapt. It's not about trying to agree with everyone. It's about making sure that the positions we take are informed positions.

Kelly: And Simon?

Allen: Simon needs to understand that we don't get to boss people about. If we try pushing people around without making any effort to understand their point of view, then they'll just cross their arms, dig their heels in and stop talking to us.

Kelly cast her mind back to her morning with the kids, Katie scowling and Stevie cross that she wouldn't follow his instructions.

Kelly: You're not the boss of me. No one is. I do what I like. (*Allen looks at her strangely.*) I agree with you that Simon's preferred way of doing things won't lead to great outcomes (*Allen nods happily.*) But when you say Simon needs to change, how is that different to Simon telling you that middle-management needs to change? (*Allen opens his mouth as if to speak before changing his mind.*)

As she walked out to the carpark, Kelly reflected on how different the complexity mindset was from other ways of thinking about systems. Depicting an organisation as if it was a computer or an aircraft engine or a living organism really didn't work. What if all the components of an aircraft engine gathered regularly in little groups and decided to reinvent themselves? What if all the cells in her heart decided they don't like pumping blood anymore? Perhaps these ways of thinking are helpful when issues are more straightforward and people more inclined to agree, but aren't all organisations complex? And don't people disagree about pretty much everything? How do you decide if a system is *not* complex?

She thought back to the Stacey Model she had been so excited by just a few weeks previous (Figure 5.2). Now it didn't make so much sense.[7] She thought of Simon, getting frustrated because Helen was spending so much time engaging with her staff. Clearly, Simon believed the organisation operated according to simple rules. Helen and Allen thought the reality was more complex. How do you decide if a system is simple, complicated or complex? There is no single, objective, source of wisdom to refer to. It's all subjective, a matter for conjecture. To even ask oneself the question is to position oneself outside the system, like some kind of objective observer. It makes no sense. There was no compass.

Hmm, she thought, food for thought. What was for lunch?

Coaching through this lens

Based on this philosophy, we might witness the following behaviours in a coach:

1 **Looking macro**

Through a complexity lens the coach is constantly attuned to people attributing outcomes to the actions of individuals. The coachee, for example, who attributes lukewarm responses to her efforts to influence, to her own inadequacy. Or the line manager who attributes disappointing performance to the capacity of individual direct reports. Or the CEO who attributes corruption to individual morals and values. I worked recently with an organisation who uncovered widespread misconduct across a large piece of the organisation. An initial collective response was to consider terminating every individual identified. Fortunately, the terminations were not actioned. A week later the organisation determined to explore in greater depth the circumstances in which the misconduct had taken place. No one was terminated. The organisation instead stepped back and considered the patterns of behaviour and how they seemed to have originated and evolved. They reframed the issue as something that had emerged from the interaction between people over time. They recognised their own role in that process and how some of the things they had said or not said, had contributed to the overall pattern.

Many leaders instinctively attribute outcomes to the behaviour of individuals. Many coaches do too. If a leader says she is getting feedback that she needs to be more animated and engaging, then my first response may be to encourage the person to go to acting classes and learn to be more animated and engaging. Through a first order lens I am seeing it as an issue for the individual and am encouraging the individual to pull a lever in the expectation of getting an immediate result. But what would I see if I were to consider more deeply my coachee's interactions with others in the system? Having worked with this business a long time, I can see that the recent economic downturn has hit the business hard. Whereas the culture before was friendly and accommodating, I can see now how behavioural patterns have shifted. Managers are being asked to make recommendations with energy and enthusiasm, because senior management members themselves are worried and looking for assurance that people will follow through on plans. I can see this happening everywhere. This may be a more useful perspective for the coachee to work with. The most useful agenda may not be about the failings of a leader who needs to be more animated and engaging. The more useful agenda may be about an organisation whose leadership are worried, who need assurance wherever they can get it. The challenge to the leader is not to be more engaging and animated necessarily. It is to develop the capacity to read the runes and respond most appropriately.

2 Looking micro

The coach will also look local. Suppose the coach was new to this organisation and had no sense of history, no sense of how behavioural patterns may have changed over time. The coach is as much in the dark about the context in which the coachee is being asked to be more animated and engaged. Either coach and coachee just take the pattern for granted and assume it's an issue for the individual (a first order perspective) or else they go looking to understand more about what's going on, in an effort to reveal factors that may be hidden from view. First and second order perspectives, and the complexity perspective, all offer different strategies for going about that task. The complexity coach encourages the coachee to go looking to understand how people in different sub-systems within the organisation as a whole are talking about what is currently required of a good leader. What new perspectives are emerging, and where are those perspectives emerging from?

In this case, again rather than focus solely on the behaviour of the individual, the coachee asks his line manager about the mood among senior managers at the moment. What conversations are taking place? In the context of declining performance, what are senior leaders saying they want middle managers to do? Who seem to be the opinion formers and thought leaders? How are they thinking? From which may emerge a picture in which Jane, the CFO, seems to have taken the lead addressing the decline in performance. She comes from a previous organisation that valued great orator skills. She is talking to whoever will listen, including the HR Director, about getting leaders further down the organisation to understand the need to speak with passion and purpose. Bob, the CEO, and Phillip, the Marketing Director, are less convinced. The coachee starts to understand how best to interact with who if he is to have the greatest impact.

3 Experiencing the system

This coach, curious to better understand the nature of local interaction, wants to experience local interaction.

The experience enables the coach to observe and understand more. So, whilst some coaches may be disinclined to interact with other stakeholders, perhaps because they feel this will impinge on their neutrality, this coach seeks out every opportunity to engage and interact. This might include three-way conversations with coachee and line manager. It might include other conversations with stakeholders. It might include spending time accompanying the coachee in their work life. Three-way conversations with stakeholders are relatively commonplace these days in organisational coaching, usually held to ensure everyone is aligned around the goals for an assignment. But the coach is less interested in attaining consensus on goals, and more interested in experiencing the relationship between coachee and line manager (and their relationships with the coach!). The coach is very much aware when interacting with the system that she is not only experiencing the system, but the system is also experiencing her. She is part of the system.

4 Exploring conflict

This coach has a different relationship with conflict. Many coaches are uncomfortable with conflict. They try to dampen it down at every opportunity. They try to avoid it, particularly when working with teams. Through a complexity lens, however, the coach goes *looking* for conflict, for at least two reasons. First, the expression of disagreement is often a question. It often represents a figurative shrug of the shoulders; 'from where I'm standing that doesn't make sense to me – help me understand'. If the leader ignores the conflicting view, or chooses to debate it, then she is choosing not to listen to the question. As Allen said, 'resistance to change' is often a misnomer for feeling the 'need to ask questions'. People don't always express their disagreement politely. This may be because they are locked in their own view; they are looking at things that you can't see. What does the view look like from their balcony? Or they may not be locked in their own view at all. They may be quite flexible and prepared to listen and engage with you., but they are used to challenging leaders who express little interest in what they have to say.

So, instead of asking a question calmly, they go straight to making a noise and waving their hands. It sounds like entrenched resistance to you, but actually it's a forlorn plea to be listened to.

The second reason the coach looks for conflict is because this is where innovation and creativity happens. The leader who looks to dampen discordance also dampens innovation. The diversity agenda is not a politically correct policy designed to appease minorities. The diversity agenda is about bringing together multiple perspectives and creating a space in which new insights are likely to emerge in service of change. No diversity, no innovation, no change. So, the complexity coach goes looking for conflict. Where she finds it, she is curious. What seems to be happening in this relationship? What is the nature of the conflict taking place? How is this tension, this conflict, useful? What purpose does it serve?

This propensity to seek out conflict is particularly important when coaching teams. In any team there exist tensions. The manifestation of those tensions may lead the team coach to feel uncomfortable, because the team will expect the coach to manage those tensions. Often those tensions are directed at the coach, as the person charged with 'holding the space'. So, we see many team coaches, facilitators and consultants discouraging the expression of tension. But if the team can 'lean into' the tension, they are able to explore the nature of the tension and understand what the tension can tell them about the dynamics of the team. The effective team coach seeks to create a safe space in which people feel better able to express tension. The effective team coach goes looking for tension in service of enabling the team to learn how to manage its dynamics more effectively.

5 Understanding self

From a complexity perspective the coach is as much an agent of change as is anyone else in the organisational system. Everything the coach says has an impact. It isn't possible to understand precisely the consequence of any specific utterance, but the coach will have an intuitive idea as to how they can most effectively behave. The outcome of any coaching assignment always depends to a great extent on the behaviour of the coach. Coaching conversations are co-created. In a dyadic conversation, coach and coachee co-create focus, meaning and insight. This means that if Julie was coaching Bob instead of me, then the outcome would be different. I am not neutral. Every word I say has an impact on the conversation. Every facial expression noticed by the coachee has an impact. Each time I decide to stay quiet, and say nothing, has an impact. I cannot hope to be neutral because there is no such thing. I am listening and responding through the lens of my experiences, beliefs and values. But I can be choiceful and purposeful. I can, in each and every moment, make a conscious choice as to what will be most useful in the moment. The more I understand my self, the more I understand where my own thoughts and potential utterances come from, the wiser will be my choices.

Leading through this lens

When asked to talk about specific events in the past or plans for the future, this leader places less emphasis on the capacity of individuals to deliver on their objectives. She still does, of course, talk about the performance of individuals, but always in the context of the wider system. The leader seems to have an uncanny intuition for what is happening where. It is evident that she gets out and about and talks to people. In any given scenario she has her eye on one or two groups of people, one or two functions, where she feels she needs to get more involved and engage in conversation. This leader is by no means stress-free because she knows that she can neither control nor reliably predict what will happen next, and some potential outcomes are not the outcomes she is looking for. So, she gives the impression of being alert, attentive to what is happening both without and within the organisation. Because not many people think in this way, it is quite possible that those more senior than her in the organisation behave as if the world operated according to first or second order principles. She recognises this and views the behaviour of her senior leaders as another aspect of the overall system, one to be reflected upon and responded to as feels most appropriate. This leader thinks deeply and relies on her intuition and the intuition of others in making decisions. She is comfortable with conflict. Unlike many in the organisation, she gives feedback to anyone she comes into contact with, so long as she feels it will be a useful thing to do. She doesn't label people or blame people. She talks in terms of her own experience of events, recognising that her perspective is but one perspective in the system. She receives feedback with calm curiosity. She asks questions, to understand where the feedback is coming from. She doesn't get upset by feedback because she doesn't see it as personal criticism. Feedback is the organisation talking, helping her understand how the system operates, in particular how it is responding to her presence in the system.

Developing leaders

I haven't come across many leadership programmes that well reflect complexity principles. Those I have come across place emphasis on how the leader thinks and not at all on generic leadership competencies. As mentioned before, many traditional leadership programmes are essentially coercive. They are based on a belief that a certain set of behaviours always leads to desirable outcomes. This is a perspective based on principles of control and predictability. Programmes based on complexity principles recognise that there is no standard set of skills and competencies that constitute outstanding leadership. Effective leaders have the capacity to assess what is needed in the moment and behave accordingly. Ralph Stacey talks about 'practical judgment', knowing how to respond in any given scenario by referring to the experience of having faced it before.[8] The task of the leadership developer is therefore to support the participant in facing new dilemmas and reflecting on her response to those dilemmas.

The organisation can help by helping the leader access different ways of thinking, different ways of relating to the world. This kind of leadership programme helps leaders recognise the futility of seeking to control outcomes, to become more comfortable with the volatility, complexity and ambiguity of an uncertain world. You cannot teach this way of thinking. You can allude to it, but to understand these principles conceptually is not the same thing as working from those principles in practice. We access new ways of thinking when old ways of thinking don't work. So, we need to create programmes framed around the work that leaders actually do. We need to walk next to leaders as they tackle complex scenarios and provide an opportunity to regularly reflect on those experiences with fellow leaders, and coaches who resist the temptation to talk about these scenarios in terms of skills and competencies.

Considering leadership development through this lens, we see a glaring paradox. Often, when times get tough, organisations cancel leadership training. Organisations don't just pick on leadership training, of course. Cost-cutting measures are applied everywhere as measures are taken to prop up profitability. These measures usually don't meet much resistance. This is how we always respond to short-falls in revenue. Leaders get on with doing things, whatever things they can think of, to generate revenue. Thinking of traditional leadership development programmes, these cuts are quite logical. Traditional leadership programmes, designed in accordance with first and second order princi-ples, usually require the participant to attend a workshop and learn some new skills which they can then apply in the workplace. These programmes are concerned with doing things. At times of crisis leaders have enough to do, and so it may make sense to defer programmes that are designed to educate them in doing things they may not have time to do. But programmes designed to enable the leader to access new ways of thinking, thinking especially required when events are particularly unpredictable, volatile and complex, should be saved for when leaders most need them. If leaders seek new ways of thinking when old ways of thinking don't work, then we should be offering these programmes at times of crisis. And providing coaches to help leaders reflect, not on materials presented in the classroom, but on events in the real world.

These leadership programmes either don't make a lot of use of multi-rater surveys, or else they position them differently. Multi-rater surveys encourage us to think of ourselves as single entities defined in terms of competencies. More and more organisations these days seem weary with these tools, recognising their limitations. Through a complexity lens, leadership may be best understood as relational. I am perceived differently by different people through different lenses. My capacity as leader is related to my capacity to discern how I am being perceived in the moment and to respond accordingly.

For example, Sue the CEO says that Brian needs to work on his communication skills. Brian is not on her team but is highly regarded. She says Brian is too direct and blunt, and the way he talks to people is demotivating them. She asks Brian to undertake a multi-rater survey, hoping it will reinforce her message. The survey provides evidence to support Sue's view. Encouraged by his coach, Brian decides he needs to change the way he speaks to people. His style changes, but people still seem disengaged.

Working with a different coach, Brian does a little research, seeking to understand better what is going on for Sue. He finds out that Sue is having problems with her team. Two people are under a lot of stress, and that stress is being directed at Sue. One person has gone on stress-leave, and it isn't clear how the situation can be resolved. The other person is still at work and has now started making formal complaints about Sue. Sue has asked HR for help. The HR person is new to the organisation and worked for a previous organisation where harmony was valued above constructive conflict. Sue, the HR person and the HR person's assistant have been spending a lot of time together and are seeking to build a micro-culture within her team where people put a lot of energy into complimenting each other's achievements and always look for the positive.

Brian begins to understand how Sue may be super-sensitive to his behaviours, afraid of stirring further discord in the organisation. Brian seeks feedback from some of his other colleagues. Some of those colleagues really value his behaviour. They like that they always know what he is thinking. His boss confesses that he finds Brian's intensity a little wearing at times. It doesn't help that his boss's wife has just given birth to twins and he isn't getting much sleep. Brian walks away from the survey process with a long list of actions, only some of which relate to his own behaviour. He pledges to invest more time in the future paying attention to what is happening around him.

At the movies

The last movie in the paper by Harri Raisio and Niklas Lundstrom is *Mr Nobody*. This movie probably better deserves the title *Chaos Theory* than does the actual movie *Chaos Theory*. The central character is Nemo, who is interviewed about his past life at the age of 118. Nemo recounts pivotal points in his life, beginning with his parents' divorce when he is aged nine, when he has to choose whether to live with his mother or father. In one scenario he chooses to live with his mother and in another scenario he chooses to live with his father, and each scenario begats a different journey and a new series of choices. In one timeline he meets Anna at age 15 but is too shy to forge a relationship. In another timeline Nemo and Anna spend time together and fall in love. The Nemo and Anna who fall in love are later separated. In one scenario they meet again and Anna gives Nemo his phone number, but he loses it. In another scenario they get married but Nemo crashes his car on the way home one night and dies. And so on. Small events have significant consequences. In one scene Nemo trips at the last moment while trying to join his mother on a train and ends up living with his father. In another scene a leaf on the road causes Nemo's car to serve into a lake, leading to his death. Anna's telephone number is obliterated by a raindrop.

At the end of the interview Nemo tells the interviewer that they are both figments of the imagination of the nine-year-old boy having to choose between his mother and father, as he runs through multiple scenarios in an effort to make a decision. The boy is also imagining a whole range of other possible scenarios at the same time, as he mulls upon what to do. In recounting his story, the events of which he is unable to control, Nemo appears happy and relaxed, unlike Evan. He embraces chaos. At the end of the film he chooses a third scenario, to live with neither his mother nor his father, an option that becomes apparent to Nemo only after having experienced all the various scenarios his life follows. He is a part of the system and co-evolves with it. He has choice as to how he behaves, but he cannot control others' responses to his behaviours.

Your 3Ps

1 What aspects of chaos and complexity theories make sense to you?
2 If you review your Purpose again now, has it changed at all?
3 What insights have you gained as to how you coach now – what is your current Practice?
4 Do you coach differently in different contexts? If so, what triggers you in each context?
5 Do you have a glimpse yet of what other practical approaches you might seek to integrate in your practice?

Segue . . .

Kelly saw it online before Allen had a chance to tell her – Shoozon had agreed to purchase BigBootz. As she read through the article, Kelly found the logic of the acquisition hard to fathom. Shoozon sold shoes direct to families – women's shoes, children's shoes, men's business shoes and shoes for leisure. BigBootz specialised in work shoes, for which the biggest customers were construction companies, manufacturing, industry, waste removal, etc. She wondered what conversations had taken place from which emerged a conviction that this was a good thing to do. She looked forward to meeting with Allen and finding out the story and to hearing how this was going to impact on him.

Notes

1 Jurassic Park. Dir. Steven Spielberg. Universal Pictures, 1993. Film.
2 Stacey, R.D. & Mowles, C. (2016). *Strategic Management and Organisational Dynamics*, 7th edition. Pearson.

3 Reynolds, C.W. (1987). Flocks, Herds and Schools: A Distributed Behaviour Model. Proceedings of Siggraph '87. *Computer Graphics, 21*(4), 25–34. Summarised in Stacey & Mowles.

4 Ray, T.S. (1992). An Approach to the Synthesis of Life. In: Langton, G.C., Taylor, C., Doyne Farmer, J. & Rasmussen, S. (Eds.), *Artificial Life II*. Sante Fe Institute, Studies in the Sciences of Complexity, 10. Addison-Wesley. Also Summarised in Stacey & Mowles.

5 Gareth Morgan explains the idea of 'strange attractors' well in *Images of Organization* – Morgan, G. (2006). *Images of Organization*. Sage.

6 Stacey, R. (2012). *Tools and Techniques of Leadership and Management: Meeting the Challenge of Complexity*. Routledge.

7 In Stacey, R. (2012). *Tools and Techniques of Leadership and Management: Meeting the Challenge of Complexity*. Routledge – Stacey himself tells the story of how he came to regret coming up with the model in the first place. In the next chapter, however, we will make a case for the value of the model.

8 Stacey, R. (2012). *Tools and Techniques of Leadership and Management: Meeting the Challenge of Complexity*. Routledge.

6

Meta-systemic

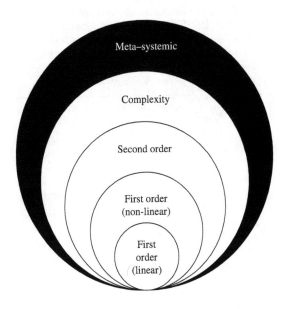

Theory in a nutshell

Ralph Stacey and complex responsive processes

There are many different versions of complexity thinking. Most focus on the behaviour of individual agents, operating in local environments or sub-systems. To further their understanding of complex systems, mathematical modelers assign rules to individual agents and observe the outcome of the interaction between those agents. But how applicable is this approach in seeking to understand the behaviour of people? People are not flocking birds, each bird following simple rules. People are conscious, emotional and spontaneous, capable of observing the pattern of interactions within which they are operating and responding accordingly. The choices people make are often neither logical nor obvious, even to themselves. People think about their work and are often bored by repetition. They may seek novelty for novelty's sake. Some dislike being told what to do, others value rules and follow those rules even if they don't make sense. The way people behave, at least in some contexts, is un-modellable, and so the system metaphor may not be useful.

Ralph Stacey and Chris Mowles[1] suggest it is more useful to focus on the responsive manner in which humans interact with each other. People don't respond according to simple rules. They don't always follow instruction. They don't always behave in a way that makes sense to other people. Therefore, we cannot always predict their behaviours, and we cannot hope to control their behaviours. This is tremendously frustrating to the leader of an organisation who believes it is his role is to direct others and that others are bound to comply. For that leader, non-compliance equals insubordination. For the leader of an organisation who believes in the overwhelming value of logic and rationality, non-compliance equals stupidity. For these leaders, leadership is about the individual. Individuals think for themselves, and by themselves, and so I can fix non-compliance by taking out the non-compliant individuals.

Stacey and Mowles suggest that notions of autonomy and independence are ultimately fictions. People make sense together. Even the individual who sits by herself in an office, paying little attention to her co-workers, thinking that the decisions she makes are wholly independent, is wrong – according to this way of thinking. We all interact with others, constantly – face-to-face, through traditional methods of communication, reading books, social media, etc. We may think we privilege the views of special others, and these indeed may be the ideas we tend to consciously integrate within our own perspectives. But the meaning we make of the world is also a function of the opinions and behaviours of those we don't consciously take on board. For example, the direct report who never submits their reports on time, and attributes it to non-cooperation on the part of others, may reinforce my belief in personal accountability.

Through this lens we look beyond the functioning of the individual to the responsive manner in which people interact with each other. If people in an organisation are interdependent, then no one person can choose what happens to all of them. Actions are not determined by individuals, but they emerge from the interactions between people. The leader's role thus becomes master influencer rather than master decider. The role of the leader is to engage intentionally and skilfully in local interaction, responding in the moment to events as they emerge. As Stacey puts it:

> All anyone can ever do, no matter how powerful, is engage intentionally, and as skilfully as possible, in local interaction.[2]

The word 'skilfully' sticks out for me. To engage in this way is as much about mindset and ways of thinking as it is about skills. To engage in this way requires studying one's own ideologies around control and the role of a leader and accessing new ideologies and ways of thinking. This leader buys into the idea that he cannot control what happens next. He is open to the idea his leadership team will continue to pull him in different directions, that he may never succeed in understanding how aspects of his organisation function. And he is open to the possibility that however insightful he feels his perspective on events might be, he may never succeed in persuading everyone, all the time, to see things the same way. And he is fine with that.

Instead of trying to see the organisation as a system, Stacey suggests instead that we focus on the responsive manner in which humans interact with each other. People are social, and the process through which they make meaning of themselves and the world in which they operate is social. To try to depict this as a system may not be useful. Ideas of systems, boundaries and sub-systems may make it unnecessarily difficult to sense what is happening. If the organisation is a 'system', it is a system too complex to understand, whose patterns, groupings and boundaries (insofar as any of these things are real) are constantly shifting and changing. That doesn't mean there is no value in seeking to understand how an organisation works. Hypotheses help us make sense of our surroundings and guide us in our actions and behaviours. And if we are astute, we will be hypothesising as to the responses our hypotheses are generating, and we will be constantly reviewing and amending our hypotheses. If we do this well, with a curious mind and a courageous voice, then we may be successful in constructively influencing outcomes. This perspective is essentially quite simple. It says that so-called leaders, like everyone else in an organisation, just need to pay attention to relationships and patterns of relationships. It is deceptively simple, with a number of implications, some of which we'll explore here and continue to explore in the next chapter with the help of Kelly and Allen.

Meta thinking

Stacey compares and contrasts the complex responsive process perspective with other ways of thinking and concludes that the complex responsive perspective is the most useful. In sharing these ideas at conferences and webinars over the last year I have experienced others too, comparing and contrasting these different ways of thinking, deciding which best reflects their own way of thinking and which they prefer. The general consensus seems to be that we coaches are all pretty much thinking in the complexity domain. At a coaching supervision conference, one participant suggested that coaches in Europe had progressed from first and second order ways of thinking and didn't talk about those philosophies anymore because they were no longer relevant. On the other hand, when I shared these ideas with a group of academic psychologists, none of whom were coaches, a man put his hand up and said he couldn't identify with this perspective. He said that in his world, in which he and his colleagues were engaged in developing new vaccines, you couldn't possibly operate other than with reference to a linear model of cause and effect. A potential vaccine either does or does not have the desired impact. The leader of the team is responsible for ensuring protocols are followed and that correct conclusions are drawn from experiments. In other words, the first order way of thinking about systems is deemed both useful and essential and other perspectives are wishy-washy and dangerous.

I don't think it is useful to categorise ourselves. We see in the corporate arena many people who think through first and second order lenses. Control is still the dominant ideology. Are we really any different? I suspect we all think through that first order lens sometimes. which is good, because if we want to communicate successfully with others and build good coaching relationships with others, we need to be able to engage through that lens. The old coaching adage, 'meet your client where they are', applies to most relationships in life, not just coaching. Second, if we believe Bateson is right in suggesting we are largely incapable of understanding the complexity of the world in which we live, then we must acknowledge our need to find simple frameworks that allow us to see the world in simple terms. All the ways of thinking we have covered in this book may be viewed as efforts to simplify that which is complex. To discard these ways of thinking is to reject ways of simplifying the complex. There is nothing wrong in simplifying the complex in order to find meaning, so long as we realise we are doing it. As a coach, do you never encourage your coachee to work out simple solutions to apparently simple predicaments, in essence colluding around a first order model of change? If my eye constantly hurts, then it may well solve the problem if I stop poking it with a sharp stick. We simplify all the time; it is how we operate. The question is, to what extent do we realise we are simplifying and holding that simplification as hypothesis?

As Kelly discovered in the last chapter, some authors offer us diagnostic frameworks, such as the Stacey Model, described earlier. These models invite us to diagnose the local environment and to categorise it.[3] If the scenario is simple, then I can apply first order thinking successfully. If it is complex, then I must think in terms of chaos theory or complex adaptive systems. How convenient and useful. But Kelly then realised the absurdity of the model when considered through a complexity lens, the idea that we can stand outside a system and come up with an objective viewpoint as to how it is functioning. Through the complexity lens the diagnosis itself emerges from the system. If the system I am scrutinising (of which I am actually a part) wishes to think of itself as simple, then I am likely to diagnose it as being simple. To diagnose the system and plot an intervention on that basis is like entering a formula into an Excel spreadsheet that includes the formula itself. If you do this, then Excel will tell you 'there are one or more circular references where a formula refers to its own cell either directly or indirectly. This might cause them to calculate incorrectly.' This is good advice to bear in mind. For which reason Stacey later regretted coming up with his model and asked others to stop citing it.

If we can't meaningfully diagnose whether a system is complex or complicated, then are we better off just assuming that everything is complex? Malcolm Higgs and Deborah Rowland published the results of research suggesting that the leadership approach that works best in emergent scenarios works best anyway in all other scenarios.[4] So why bother trying to diagnose a scenario? Why not just assume it is always complex? In some situations this may be a useful approach. In others, less so. In still other situations it may be useful to think through first and second order lenses, and/or a complexity lens. First, because it enables us to communicate with others who think through that lens. If you approach an organisation whose leadership programmes are designed to first order principles, you are unlikely to persuade the owner of that programme to throw out skills workshops and leadership competency frameworks by lecturing them on complexity theories. If you wish to influence that individual, then you need to understand their frame of reference and be able to speak to that frame of reference. Second, these frames of reference sometimes makes sense. If the pharmacist/psychologist finds the first order perspective useful; if OD professionals find second order philosophies useful; if the complexity coach finds the idea of systems, sub-systems and boundaries useful, then why should we object? So long as they are useful. Some people use the Stacey Model in ways that again seem useful. I can think of only one risk, which is that people consider the view through these different lenses to be 'true'. So long as we regard all of these models as metaphor, then they may have important roles to play in helping us emerge from thinking about complexity with intention and purpose.

For these reasons I haven't called this way of thinking 'complex responsive'. This way of thinking is very much based on the principles of complex responsive processes, but I am not positioning it as something distinct and separate. Rather, I am positioning it as another way of thinking, a way of thinking that recognises the value of metaphor, and thereby recognises the value of all the other ways of thinking, so long as we hold them also as metaphor. To conceive of the organisation as a hot water system, or a living system, or as system and sub-system operating to complexity principles – these may all be useful metaphors in some circumstances. So, this is the 'Meta' way of thinking about systems. Meta here means meta-systemic, adopting a meta-perspective and appreciating the value of meta-phor. We are giving ourselves permission to play with any of these philosophies and frameworks in engaging with people and how they interact. So long as we recognise that the idea of organisation-as-system is a metaphor, that it isn't 'true', and that there is always a risk of becoming overly attached to a single model, framework or theory.

Some people find the meta-perspective challenging. People become very attached to their own personal perspectives and consider them to be 'right' and 'truthful'. I have experienced this over the last couple of years in preparing to write this book – for example, the person who got cross with me because I wasn't compelled by the idea of labelling the first order perspective systematic rather than systemic. Or the person who gave me a lecture on the reality of organisations and boundaries. We like things to be 'real'.

Philosophy

Summarising the previous section, a coach operating to Meta principles is likely to adopt all or some of the following beliefs:

1 Perspective on system

There are some senses in which organisations are real and some senses in which they are not. They are real in that many people have contracts with legal entities that oblige them to perform certain duties in return for remuneration. They are real in that people who have signed such contracts with the same entity often find themselves working in the same physical location. They are real in that we talk about organisations a lot, we tell stories about organisations and we attribute much that happens in our world to the functioning of organisations. Through this lens, they are not real in much other sense. We talk about organisations as if there exist hard boundaries between the people working for that organisation and those who don't. There are no such boundaries. We talk about organisations as if they have a single purpose, a common set of values, a unified intention, a common culture. They don't. We talk about organisations as if they have a character of their own. Some banks, for example, are mean and nasty. Some telecoms companies don't listen. Oil companies don't care about climate change. But organisations are not living entities.

Through this lens, organisations are not systems because organisations are not real. An airplane engine is real. A living system, such as the human body, is real. An organisation is not real. It is a metaphor. Ralph Stacey and Chris Mowles say:[5]

> Organisations are not things at all, let alone living things. They are processes of communication and joint action. Communication and joint action as such are not alive. It is the bodies communicating and interacting that are alive.

This is a big pill to swallow. What do you mean organisations are not real? We read about organisations all the time. Organisations have share prices. They employ people. But the 'organisation' can be seen as just a story we tell ourselves, a story that we co-create together. We talk about this organisation as if it is real and has a character of its own. This character, this story, emerges through conversation. People who work for the same company as I are not the only people who participate in that meaning-making process. Customers, suppliers, joint-venture partners, regulators, media, my ten-year-old daughter and the bloke in the pub are all participants in the process.

If organisations are not systems, then there are no sub-systems either. To talk about the individual nested within the team, nested within the division, nested within the organisation, nested within the economy, nested within society, etc., is just a story. It may be a useful story, but it's just a story. If I am in the park and I see the employees of ABC Ltd all having a barbecue, I may feel a boundary between us. They work for ABC Ltd and I don't. But the boundary is a figment of my imagination. I can walk up to them, open a beer and start talking. I can walk straight through the boundary as if it isn't there. Because it isn't.

So, if there are no systems, and no sub-systems, then there are no real boundaries. True, I can't get into your office without a pass, and you can. But this not a hard boundary when it comes to meaning making. Many people in an organisation don't work in the office. They work at home or spend their time visiting clients. They go to conferences and go to cafés and go out to dinner. Even if they work in an office 16 hours a day, five days a week, they talk to people on the phone, communicate by text and email, and browse the internet. And if you go to the offices of any particular organisation, you will likely come across people employed by other legal entities; contractors, consultants and joint-venture partners, for example. The same is true when we talk about the marketing department and what a good job they are doing in contrast to the IT department. What does this really mean? That a group of people, some of whom are employees of the legal entity and some of whom often are not, have been interacting with each other and with people employed by other legal entities and with other people in the same organisational entity, including people who are called IT people. And from those interactions has emerged a set of outcomes that are adjudged by others in the organisation to have been successful.

Through the Meta-lens, the limitation of some complexity thinking is that it over-privileges the organisation-as-system. We can talk about an organisation in terms of different departments, different markets and countries, and represent these in terms of sub-systems. We can look outside the organisation and represent the external environment in terms of sub-systems: customers, suppliers, government, media and so on. These may be useful representations of the world, or they may not. But they are not real. Organisations are not real, they are not systems, they don't have sub-systems. If we assume that systems are real, then this may cloud our thinking, blinker us to aspects of what is happening around us. The meta-systemic coach is happy to talk about organisations and boundaries so long as we remember that these notions are, to a great extent, fictions. We just need to be careful we don't limit our exploration of events to those interactions taking place within these fictional boundaries.

2 Perspective on people

Tatiana Bachkirova and Simon Borrington wrote a paper about beautiful ideas that can make us ill.[6] The paper critiques narratives around positive psychology, mindfulness and transformational coaching. To that list we might add the idea of 'autonomy'. Positional power is but one form of power, through which the leader cannot hope to control all outcomes. Change is constant, unpredictable and, to a great extent, emergent. Creating expectations of individuals that they can control outcomes in this environment isn't good for the individual concerned. Burdened with such expectation, they will likely experience stress and anxiety. As will everyone else who looks to this leader to deliver them from mediocrity. The idea of autonomy may be the unhealthiest idea of all, the antithesis to how change actually happens. It may be more fruitful to talk about responsibility and the responsibility of the individual to play a role as self-aware participant in the emergence of change.

There is no duality through the meta-lens. Even through a complexity lens, there is a temptation to stand outside the organisation and diagnose how it is functioning. Models such as the Stacey Model are examples of this. These models are useful, but they don't represent reality. Every person in an organisation has an impact on events through every conversation they have. And that includes leaders. Leaders may not get to control outcomes, but they certainly influence outcomes, intentionally or otherwise, and often in ways they do not intend.

3 Perspective on change Conflict and change

In many teams, in many organisations, conflict is framed as undesirable. Anyone perceived to be regularly engaging in conflict may be experienced as being awkward or difficult. At the same time, many organisations are seeking to become more diverse, especially in terms of gender and ethnicity, and more innovative. To truly value diversity and to foster innovation is to welcome a broader range of perspective, which inevitably means disagreement. We can attempt to differentiate between constructive conflict and destructive conflict, and that seems useful up to a point. It is clearly possible to disagree with what someone is saying whilst at the same time respecting the individual for the value they bring, but these kinds of distinction will always remain to a large degree subjective. If, for example, I am senior to you and I harbour a belief that junior staff should always agree with the views expressed by their superiors, then I will feel disrespected by any kind of challenge, no matter how it is expressed. If I feel that to contradict someone in public, in front of other people, without giving people time to think through a response, is disrespectful, then again, no matter what you say, I will feel disrespected if you disagree with me in public. And so, some organisations play safe, which likely inhibits their capacity to respond effectively to change.

Successful organisations recognise that in a complex, ever-changing world, no one person will ever know everything that is going on. We therefore need to seek multiple perspectives, and preferably multiple versions of each perspective, recognising that we all look at the world through different lenses. If organisations are to successfully navigate complexity, there needs to be a process through which multiple perspectives may be held and considered. Notice that conflicts of perspective exist whether we surface them or not. The question is – do we want to surface conflict so that we can work with it, and ultimately benefit from it? Or do we wish to suppress it? In the latter case it won't go away; it will simply find other outlets, contributing to the further spreading of 'organisational fault-lines'.[7] An organisational fault-line is a metaphor, to represent the felt existence of a barrier between one or more local communities in any organisation.

If two people come together with the exact same philosophy and beliefs, then no change will emerge from that interaction. If the leader wants to influence change, therefore, he/she has to *seek out* conflict. This is an argument for diversity, not only in terms of gender, age, ethnic background, etc., but in every aspect. Diversity, from this perspective, is an agenda that is absolutely fundamental to the success of any organisation in a VUCA world. Organisations whose executive teams are all middle-aged white men won't succeed. Such a perspective places the onus on organisations to find ways of supporting 'difficult conversations'. People have to be brilliant at having these kinds of conversation if the 'organisation' is to succeed. Meantime, many of us avoid conflict and tell ourselves we are not going to get involved in 'politics'.

Dialogue and change
Change is emergent. It emerges from the myriad of conversations that people have every day across any organisation. The more dialogic the conversation, the more likely all perspectives will be heard. We're not talking about compromise. Compromise is when parties to a conversation take non-negotiables into a conversation. What emerges will be some solution that satisfies all those non-negotiables. In dialogue, all parties arrive without non-negotiables. They arrive prepared to give full consideration to any suggestion and to voice what's going on for them in the moment. Dialogue is a creative process where ideas build upon ideas. Dialogue requires that participants suspend prejudice and certainty. It requires that we listen with open minds. It requires the building of trust.

When introduced to the notion of dialogue, people often express an initial interest, then ask how they can ensure the other person commits to dialogue as well. Some theorists shrug their shoulders and agree. You can't force others to engage in dialogue, and therefore dialogue cannot be a route to facilitating change. People come to conversations with non-negotiables, and they come ready to exercise their personal power to ensure those non-negotiables are not ignored. David Bohm (quantum physicist) goes so far to say, "there is no place in the dialogue for the principle of authority and hierarchy".[8] He suggests that there is no purpose or agenda in pure dialogue, that dialogue is "an empty place, where we can let anything be talked about." Organisations are, however, full of purpose, and there is little appetite for sitting down with people in an empty space to talk about whatever comes into people's minds.

But this, it seems to me, is quite a binary view, the view that you are engaged in dialogue or you are not, and because power dynamics exist, this means that few people ever listen with a completely open mind, and dialogue in organisations is impossible. This is a useful view, in that it reminds us that change does not emerge only from dialogue. Change emerges from interactions between people, regardless of the way in which they relate. But dialogue is nevertheless a useful construct for a leader. It encourages us to create spaces for people to listen to each other with as open a mind and heart as possible. They may not be engaged in pure dialogue. They may fail to engage in dialogue at all. But the greater the effort people make to hear the perspectives of others, and to frame their own contributions as subjective and fallible, the richer the conversation, and the more considered the outcomes of that conversation.

Politics and change

Some leaders say they don't like 'playing politics', but 'playing politics' is what is required to navigate the complexity of interpersonal relationships that sits at the heart of all organisations. To choose not to play politics is to choose not to influence. Here are some dictionary definitions of the word 'politics':

- A particular set of political beliefs or principles.
- The activities associated with the governance of a country or area, especially the debate between parties having power.
- The principles relating to or inherent in a sphere or activity, especially when concerned with power and status.
- Activities aimed at improving someone's status or increasing power within an organisation.

Three themes emerge from these definitions;

1 Different people have different beliefs and values.
2 To work together effectively, people must find a way of managing differences in beliefs and values. Often people seek to manage those differences through debate.
3 People with power have a better chance of getting their way than people without power.

These themes go some way to explaining why some people dislike engaging in politics. First, whilst debate is sometimes an effective and appropriate form of conversation, at other times it speaks to a form of conflict in which people engage aggressively without respect. Many people don't enjoy that kind of conflict. Second, politics is often about the acquisition, leveraging and exercising of power. Some people are perceived to be primarily driven to enhancing their personal power. When this happens, it is often at the expense of other people's reputations, and so, again, many people seek to avoid these kinds of interaction.

We can't pretend that politics doesn't often entail debate and the pursuit of individual power, but if we are to enhance our capacity to influence change, then we (as leaders and coaches) must deepen our understanding as to the nature of power within specific organisations and speculate as to how we can best influence patterns of relating. The leader who says that she doesn't like to engage in politics is unlikely to be successful. The leader who says she will let her results speak for her may be overlooked.

People respond to us based on their perception of us. We are experienced by lots of people who compare their experiences of us with each other. A story emerges that defines both who we are and the extent to which we can be influential. If we want to be influential, we need to be aware of the story-telling process and engage in that process. I coached someone once who was directed to coaching because he was 'Dutch'. Dutch, in this instance, was shorthand for being blunt, direct and aggressive. His CEO wanted him to be less blunt, direct and aggressive. The CEO was concerned because the story of his behaviour was becoming entrenched. The story equated perceived behaviours with being Dutch. The individual concerned could have focussed on changing his behaviour, but to what extent would this have changed the story? One possibility is that he would have become the Dutchman who decided to try to be less Dutch, his new behaviours belying his pervading Dutchness. Or he might have succeeded in adopting a more overtly inquisitive and respectful way of engaging with others and become the Prodigal Dutchman. Most likely different parts of the social network would have co-created different stories, based on local experience and interpretation of his behaviour. This would include communities who would have created negative stories, because they had appreciated his open and transparent communication style and now mourned its loss. It was clear that if he wanted to progress further in the organisation, he would need to build a deeper understanding of which communities experienced him in what ways and take steps to try to influence the telling of those stories in each of those communities. He would have to engage in 'politics' because 'politics' reflects the way change happens, like it or not. Leaders don't get to choose whether or not to engage in politics. They do engage in politics. What the leader doesn't say is as important as what she does say. Politics just is. The question for the leader is how purposeful she chooses to be, and how much energy she is prepared to engage in relationships, in order to influence desired outcomes.

4 Perspective on Power

Gareth Morgan says it is a shame that many people see politics as dysfunctional.[9] The idea of politics, he says, comes from a view that says society needs to provide a means by which people with divergent interests can come together to reconcile their differences. Politics for Plato was a means of creating order without resorting to totalitarianism. Politics in a sense is the exercising of power. There are many forms of power,[10] and the potential complexity of power dynamics in an organisation is daunting. Again, the complexity thinker will be attuned to patterns of power at the macro level and to understanding how power dynamics play out at the micro level.

First and second order thinking over-privileges positional power. Positional power on its own is rarely sufficient for senior leaders to drive change down through an organisation. Such attempts may appear initially successful, but initial success usually gives way to inertia and intransigence. The invasion of Iraq springs to mind. The USA declared war on March 20, 2003, and declared victory on May 1, 2003, only to then find itself engaged in a long intractable battle against insurgency. The USA finally withdrew troops in 2011, eight years after victory was declared, leaving behind a country still locked in sectarian violence. This is not to say positional power isn't important. Of course it is. But there are other forms of power.

To attempt to influence change in a complex organisation requires a perspective on who is talking to whom and on patterns of conversation. It also requires a perspective on power. In thinking about power, we need to think beyond the obvious. We need to think beyond positional power. In company X, the IT director decided to replace an in-house legacy system with an outsourced system. The changeover would result in many IT employees being dismissed, because their knowledge of the legacy system would become valueless. Nevertheless, their cooperation would be essential if the company was going to operate effectively during the 12 months it would take to switch from one system to another. In the event their importance wasn't sufficiently appreciated, legacy system experts picked on functionality that the new system couldn't replicate and persuaded some in the business that this lack of functionality would render the new systems useless. They failed to turn up to meetings, they failed to document key aspects of the current system and they bad-mouthed the executive. The transition programme took six months longer than planned, during which system outages were commonplace, and the new system failed to deliver on some key outcomes.

Company Y was a financial company that decided to go open plan, including the CEO and the executive team. People fought to retain their offices, and the change management team had to ask the CEO to ring people up to tell them that they were not going to get an office. The Funds Managers pushed back, threatening to leave the company and take their clients with them. The CEO relented. By the time the office design was complete, the CEO and his executive were working open plan. The Funds Managers still had offices.

In company Z, a senior leader was seconded to Head Office as part of his career development plan. High potential leaders were brought into roles for 12–24 months, often heading up teams of staff who worked permanently in more junior roles. His deputy had been in the role for several years and wasn't interested in changing the way he worked. He had a great relationship with all the key stakeholders at Head Office, and those stakeholders didn't want to upset him because they got exactly what they needed from him. The incoming leader found he got no support from internal stakeholders in seeking to achieve what he'd been asked to do. Those stakeholders continued to talk to his deputy and make decisions without his involvement.

The Meta-coach recognises all of this and encourages the leader to be as effective as they can be in their myriad interactions. To recognise the nature of relationships in which they are engaging, or by which they are influenced. To recognise the presence of power, all forms of power – and not just positional power; expert power, network power, relationship power, resource power, etc. – and to consider all forms of power in deepening his navigation of social networks. She understands that social networks are complex and unpredictable and that change cannot be directed. There can never be any guarantee that a change leader will achieve the outcomes they are looking for. There is no magic pill. What leaders can do, nevertheless, is notice patterns of conversation, engage in some of those conversations to better understand how they work, hypothesise where the sources of power are and how they are being exercised, and hypothesise ways forward based on connecting the right people with each other to engage in conversation. The journey forward is always based on hypothesis, and the reformulation of hypothesis is based on learned experience.

5 Perspective on Team Coaching

When we talk about team coaching, we are straightaway assuming a boundary – the boundary between people in the team and outside the team. The team is talked about as if it is something real. Some coaches encourage teams to delay team coaching if the team is unstable, with people still coming and going. The team has a history and a reputation in the organisation. It has objectives and a purpose. But a team is not a real entity. A team is an imaginary construct. Often the composition of the team is uncertain, and so we strive harder to find the rationale that enables us to define the 'team'.

People often say that team coaching is harder than individual coaching because when you coach a team of, say, eight people, you are coaching 36 relationships instead of two. From a meta-perspective, there is no fundamental difference. Whether I am coaching an individual or I am coaching a team, the coach is working with people located in an incredibly complex network, the properties of which neither the coach nor the people being coached will ever completely understand. In a more practical sense, of course, in team coaching you have to work with, say, eight bodies in a room at once. But don't assume that what happens in the room is solely a function of the relationships in the room. For example, John the CEO and Mary the CFO are both in the room. They don't seem to be getting on very well today. John seems to be cross with Mary. You wonder if the tension in their relationship is being projected onto you, and if that is why you are feeling uncomfortable. You wonder where the tension in their relationship is coming from. You look around the room to see who else may be playing a role in their dynamic. But of course, the dynamic is not limited to the people in the room. It may be a key client, a supplier or one of their spouses who is contributing to the tension in their relationship. The coach looking through the meta-lens is hyper-aware that teams are no more real than organisations. They are (sometimes) useful constructs we use to simplify things enough that we can understand them and move on and do things.

Team coaching is becoming more popular, but it is still very new. As with all new disciplines, the market is now crowded with different people offering different definitions of coaching, often while simultaneously selling training programmes based on a particular methodology. Having attended some of those programmes myself, and indeed having taught team coaching on a university programme, I find myself curiously unmoved by many of those offerings. I also find myself feeling increasingly discomfited by the accompanying mantra that goes something like this:

> Coaching individuals is a waste of time and indeed can be destructive. Individuals don't operate in isolation and so we need to focus on coaching groups and teams instead.

On the face of it, this assertion seems to make sense. Both complexity and meta-perspectives warn us against a belief that says we can change organisations one person at a time. Such perspectives would appear to push us toward spending more time coaching groups and teams. But this mantra is too simplistic and diverts our attention from the crux of the issue. The crux of the issue is that in order to work more effectively, whatever the work we do, we need to access different ways of thinking. To push people into shifting their energies from individual coaching to group and team coaching will not of itself achieve that. The message is too binary and too simplistic.[11] If I am thinking from a complexity or meta-perspective, then I am not coaching the individual in isolation. Other stakeholders are involved in the process. I may be escorting the coachee around his workday or convening meetings with his colleagues to provide feedback. I am aware that I, as coach, am but one person in the coachee's universe. I am aware that my coachee is engaged in conversation with lots of people, all of whom are contributing to his or her meaning making. I can challenge the way my coachee is thinking, and I can challenge the way others are thinking, those with whom I come into contact. As someone coaching an individual, I know I am part of the broader system or network, and that everything I do is having an impact at some level. If I am thinking systemically, then, I would assert, I can make just as significant a contribution to my coachee and the 'organisation' for whom he/she works as can a team coach.

From a meta-perspective, encouraging people to learn a particular team coaching methodology, on the basis that the espoused process is somehow the same as thinking differently, achieves little. The team coach who is thinking solely through a first or second order lens, will be constantly propping up the same thinking in the teams with whom he is working. He is co-creating a way of thinking that is unlikely to always lead to success. He is covertly encouraging people to think about the 'team' as if it is a real entity, boundaried from other people in the same broader network. With reference back to Gregory Bateson, instead of encouraging individuals to think they know more than they do, and to charge forward purposefully and destructively, the coach is now encouraging *groups* of people to come together to charge forward. His impact therefore may be exponentially more destructive.

What concerns me about many team coaching models is that they are being offered as something real and ultimate. The team coach arrives with a reputation for knowing what a team needs to do in order to be more effective. That reputation may be why the coach was picked in the first place. It is not easy to sell an approach to working with teams based on complexity principles. And so, the team is now in the hands of the expert team coach, talking wise words about what it means to be 'systemic', a team coach who is focussed on helping people to work together more effectively within first and second order paradigms. I think this is why some programmes I have attended have left me cold. Most of them have talk about the importance of thinking systemically, without defining in any great detail what that means. I would argue that every coach is systemic, in that she is always on the lookout for causal relationships, and she understands the need to look beyond the dyadic individual coach relationship. But what the educator really means by being systemic is rarely spelt out in detail or put into any theoretical context. Instead team coaches leave the programme with a ring binder full of techniques which will help them to satisfy their clients, most of whom think through first and second order lenses.

If you are interested in the complexity and meta ways of thinking about systems, and you are planning to do more team coaching, then please pay attention to team coaching offerings. To what extent are they focussed on practice – playbooks full of techniques and models? To what extent do they appear to address philosophy? Ask people to explain their philosophies.

We don't change the way we think overnight. Adult development theory offers us some clues in this space. Indeed, there are some obvious crossovers between systems theories and adult development theories. Am I, for example, more likely to be able to access meta-philosophies if I am able to access self-transforming thinking? If I look at the world predominantly through a first order lens, then that will be my go-to when totally immersed in another's perspective, or under time pressure, or feeling stressed. To integrate different ways of thinking into my self-as-coach, as something more than a conceptual abstraction, will require me to take little steps, try out new approaches, and make time to reflect on what happened. This process can't be recreated in a one week workshop. In a one week workshop I can learn new techniques. To learn how to think differently requires me to consider my current thinking patterns. It requires me to consider new approaches and theories. It requires me to put some of that thinking into action and to reflect upon the outcomes of that action. It may require me along the way to reconsider my very purpose as a coach. This is all very different to booking into a one week workshop, hoping to come out of it as a 'systemic team coach'

From a complexity or meta-perspective, the real challenge as coach or team coach is working with human relationships. Change emerges from the interaction between components at local levels of a system (complexity) and/or between people in a network (meta). In which case, if you want to be a team coach as opposed to a 'consultant' or 'facilitator' (depending on how you define these terms), then you may choose to pay particular interest to team coaching models that explicitly include a consideration of team dynamics. But coaching individuals through a complexity or meta-lens, you likely feel the need to understand group dynamics anyway.

The team coach, like any coach thinking through this lens, is aware of the impact of power on the functioning of interpersonal dynamics. The team coach will not only focus on the way people in the room are relating, and how they are relating with those outside the room, but also on the nature of power, and how different forms of power are intertwined with the functioning of those dynamics.

There are many different ways to work with groups and teams, and I would encourage people to explore as many as they have the energy for. But ultimately I would suggest that the way a team coach thinks will ultimately determine the coach's impact. Perhaps the greatest benefit to the coach in engaging in team coaching is that team coaching will inevitably stretch us and make it more likely we can access new ways of thinking that will prove useful to us in every domain in which we operate.

Purpose

Like the complexity coach, a coach thinking through this lens is bound to pay attention to patterns of behaviour across networks and the relationships between people. Change emerges from the interactions between people, interactions fuelled by different sources of power. The coach may talk about systems or sub-systems but, when doing so, is using the idea of system as a metaphor, to direct the listener's attention to particular parts of the broader social network. The coach may express their purpose in terms of raising people's collective awareness of the functioning of the networks within which they operate, in service of behaving more purposefully and effectively within those networks. Every conversation that takes place in a network has potential significance.

Practice

Kelly and Allen

Allen looked flustered again. He confessed he had intended to postpone the session but was so busy he forgot. Rather than take a slow progressive approach, Shoozon had decided to integrate BigBootz quickly. As part of the process he had been promoted (much to his surprise) and was now looking after both product ranges. This was particularly challenging given that BigBootz's channels to market were quite different. Yet significant economies of scale had been built into the business case and approved by the Board. Even the two online channels were set up quite differently. BigBootz managed their own channel, while Shoozon outsourced the running of their website to a third party, an arrangement that was contracted for another 18 months. Allen stuck his fingers in the air and started counting off the things he needed to do.

Allen: understand the customer base, understand distribution channels, get a copy of the existing marketing strategy, meet the team, get to know the new leadership team, find out in more detail what's expected of us, challenge some of the assumptions underpinning the numbers I've been told we have to deliver . . .

Kelly: Lots to do.

Allen: You're telling me. And the plan numbers are totally unrealistic. But if these numbers are built into the acquisition business case, then they'll be impossible to shift. I don't have any idea who put the business case together or who to talk to.

Kelly: How does the new organisation work?

Allen: I have a copy of the organisation chart, but it doesn't tell me a lot. I've heard on the grapevine that some of the new leadership team are unhappy with their new roles and are looking to exploit some of the ambiguities around role boundaries to expand their influence. I'm not even sure who I'm supposed to be reporting to – two of the leadership team have asked to sit down with me and go through what I'm currently doing. I heard this morning that the team looking after the BigBootz online distribution channel is being made redundant, so they're unlikely to collaborate. And I had a call this morning from a client I've never met asking me if now was a good time to renegotiate their contract. Apparently they are BigBootz's second biggest customer, but the client manager has just resigned.

Kelly: Wow.

Allen: Wow, yes. We're now a bigger organisation. BigBootz also has distribution contracts overseas. I have no idea what to do next. Any ideas?

Yes, Kelly thought – I need some supervision. Meantime, she asked questions and helped Allen continue to explore the new scenario.

Kelly had already scheduled a first meeting with Jane, a supervisor who came highly recommended. Jane had many years' experience working in big multinational organisations, and she signed up to work with Kelly for six months. In their first session, Kelly outlined the issues as she understood them, and explained what she and Allen had been working on so far. She explained her understanding of first order and second order systems thinking and what she understood of complex adaptive systems. Jane listened carefully and asked lots of good questions. About halfway through the conversation, Jane offered to share her perspective on systems theories.

Jane: My view is that we need to hold all these systems theories lightly.

Kelly: What do you mean?

Jane: I mean that an organisation simply isn't a system in the same way that everything else we call a system is. Organisations are different.

Kelly: How are they different?

Jane: Well, you've already pointed out the limitations of first order systems theories. They imply that we can understand events in terms of simple, straightforward cause and effect. They imply we can chart out exactly how organisations operate. Second order theories take that into account, by suggesting we will never truly understand the way a system operates, and so we need to seek out multiple perspectives in deciding how we think the 'system' is operating. What they don't do is help us to understand how organisations work. But they nevertheless assume it's OK to stand apart from a 'system' and plot interventions to shift its functioning.

Kelly: I'm with you so far. But what about complexity theory? Theories of complex adaptive systems, for example? What's your opinion?

Jane: Fundamentally different, in that they focus on local activity. The basic premise is that individual agents operating in groups, in a system, interact with each other to create local outcomes, and that the interactions between different groups creates an unpredictable overall pattern, which local agents and groups then respond to, etc.

Kelly: That's my understanding. It makes sense.

Jane: It makes a lot of sense. However, like all systems theories, it too can be critiqued.

Kelly: How so?

Jane: The systemic approach inevitably means trying to understand how the system works. Mathematicians, for example, try to replicate the functioning of complex adaptive systems by assigning rules to local agents, inevitably quite simple rules.

Kelly: Simple rules means first order?

Jane: Exactly. There's an inherent paradox in there somewhere – trying to predict something on the one hand that you acknowledge is unpredictable on the other.

Kelly: Can't it help, though?

Jane: All theories can help, and if they do help, let's use them, rather than dismiss them for being theoretically unsound. But I do think we need to hold them lightly, especially when talking about social networks.

Kelly: Why social networks especially?

Jane: To be able to model precisely the behaviour of a human being, then, we would have to have a complete understanding of what it is to be human – and we don't. And human beings are not passive agents, Kelly. Imagine you work with Allen and his team and, between you, you succeed in modelling the behaviour of his team as one of these local groups.

Kelly: OK.

Jane: Right, so you succeed in working out how Allen's team interacts, and you begin to understand some of the patterns that emerge from those interactions. Well now those patterns are all visible to everyone to see, and that very understanding is likely to result in some of those people changing the way they relate to others, deliberately or otherwise. Human beings are conscious and complex and unpredictable. You, the coach, have just caused things to shift. Anyone can do it. Think of the butterfly's wings.

Kelly: I thought that was chaos theory.

Jane: It is, but that doesn't mean it isn't a useful metaphor. That's what I'm saying. All these theories have something to offer – they may provide insight. But don't get too wrapped up in the idea of organisation as system. Organisations cannot be directly compared to any kind of system. The functioning of social 'systems' will always be unpredictable and uncontrollable.

Kelly: OK. So, organisations are not systems. But it might sometimes be useful to think of them as systems.

Jane: And sometimes not.

Kelly: So, what do I tell Allen?

Kelly and Allen discuss boundaries

At their next session, Kelly asked Allen if she could come to a team meeting so she could observe directly how the team was responding to the new world. Allen agreed. He said he wouldn't have time to talk to her about what he planned to do at the meeting, but he would value her feedback. The meeting lasted for two hours and was so full of fascinating interactions that Kelly insisted they spend a full session afterwards debriefing.

Allen: What did you notice?

Kelly: There was lots going on there, Allen. Let me focus first on the general approach you took. How would you describe that?

Allen: I thought about some of the things we'd talked about in terms of systems. The importance of giving feedback, of noticing what might be going on, and the value of attending to local interactions.

Kelly: OK. And how did that show up in the way you interacted with the team?

Allen: I wanted to provide people with a clear picture of what was going on and what we needed to do. I wanted to get them to talk to me and provide them with feedback on what I was hearing.

Kelly: So, when James, the guy heading up the BigBootz online distribution channel, told you he didn't think you should bundle together the BigBootz channel with the Shoozon channel?

Allen: Well, I'm pretty sure he's worried about his team being made redundant, so I wanted to put him straight on that one.

Kelly: You told him no decision has been made.

Allen: That's the truth. The redundancy thing is currently just a rumour.

Kelly: He didn't seem very reassured.

Allen: I told him all there was to tell. At least he knows I'll always let him know what's happening.

Kelly: And what's your truth?

Allen: What do you mean?

Kelly: Do you think the business needs James and his team moving forward?

Allen: We certainly need that expertise somewhere in the system. Even if we outsource their system eventually, it will be really important to have that expertise on our side of the relationship. And we may need a multifaceted strategy anyway, particularly when you think of some of the new segments and new markets the Board has talked about.

Kelly: I didn't hear you say any of that.

Allen: It's too early to be having those conversations just yet, and I don't want to create false expectations.

Kelly: Then you asked him to cooperate with everyone and give others access to his insights and expertise.

Allen: That's what needs to happen. I need him to start behaving differently. I need to shift the way the team is currently operating, particularly when it comes to online distribution. If I can shift that part of the system, then that will be a massive win for us.

Kelly: How did you interpret his response?

Allen: He didn't say much, but I hope he took on the message. We'll find out soon, I guess. What else did you notice?

Kelly: I saw you full of confidence and determination.

Allen: That's good. I didn't feel confident.

Kelly: You talked about the rationale for the acquisition, insofar as you understand it, and you talked about what you expect from his team members. But I wonder whether you noticed everything that was happening in the room.

Allen: Like what?

Kelly: Two of the three BigBootz managers sat together quite a distance apart from James, the online distribution guy. What's happening there?

Allen: I don't know.

Kelly: They didn't say much, and I think they may have been frustrated by your apparent reluctance to talk about what reasonable sales targets might look like. They were quiet in there, but they'll talk about it, alright. In the canteen, at the local café and via email. You aren't going to be privy to any of that unless you start showing more interest in what they think.

Allen: I know what they think. They want answers, but I don't have answers to give.

Kelly: You have plenty to give, if you choose to. You could give them your attention and you could be clear with them what you do know and what you don't know.

Allen: I don't want to encourage them to speculate, and I don't want them to become even more worried about what might happen.

Kelly: So, you want them to carry on as normal until you do have something to share. You don't want to rock the boat and shake things up.

Allen: Correct.

Kelly: So, you have a picture in your head of the BigBootz folk operating like a little standalone system, with boundaries around it that you don't want to cross?

Allen: Yes, I guess so. And if we think about the complexity model we talked about, I don't want to be interjecting uncertainty into that little system, not yet. Not until I have something constructive to offer.

Kelly: But what if they aren't a little system with boundaries? What if there are no boundaries? What would that mean?

Allen: It would mean they're talking to people outside of their group. Hearing all the rumours, coming up with their own interpretations of those rumours, making up stories . . . (*Looks worried.*) OK. Let's talk about what else I could do.

Kelly and Allen discuss dialogue

A couple of weeks later, Kelly and Allen reconvene. Allen is looking guilty.

Allen: I lost my cool with Deborah, the CFO.

Kelly: Oh, dear.

Allen: Yes. I asked her to sanction our business plan for next year. I did some thinking about networks. Mark, the CEO, always seeks out her opinion. If she's onside, you know you'll get what you need. If she's not onside, then doesn't matter what support you have from others, it won't happen.

Kelly: What happened?

Allen: I called her an obstacle.

Kelly: That's not good.

Allen: I got frustrated. We arranged to meet for an hour. When I arrived, she said she only had 45 minutes. I went through the plan and she said that I had little chance of getting the cost budget that I needed, that I would have to cut it by 30%.

Kelly: What happened then?

Allen: Look, I was listening, like you told me to. I repeated back everything she said and I listened for who she was as a person, and it became apparent to me that she's an obstacle. All she does is say no. She just went straight to cutting budget, that's all she was interested in.

Kelly: (*Head in hands.*) So you called her an obstacle?
Allen: She wasn't happy.
Kelly: And where was respect in all of this?
Allen: (*Sheepish.*) I think frustration got the better of me. I lost touch with the respect bit. I just assumed she doesn't really care, that she just wants to keep her own job straightforward and simple, that she's incapable of looking beyond policy and rules.
Kelly: Hmm. Tell me what respect means to you.
Allen: It means always holding out the possibility that the person you are speaking to is on your side, that they want the best for you. That their view on life is just as valid as yours – it's just different. I don't often think like that. I spend more time thinking about avoiding conflict. Conflict breaks down relationships and makes collaboration much harder. So, I tend to self-edit rather than tune into 'respect'. Then sometimes I just get frustrated and I say it anyway, that disrespectful thing I've been sitting on.
Kelly: Frustration doesn't help.
Allen: No. When I'm frustrated, I start blaming others for slowing things down. Respect goes out the window.
Kelly: So what next?
Allen: I'm going to talk to Deborah again.

The next day, as Allen approached Deborah's desk, he promised himself to engage in respectful dialogue. He would have another go at the listening thing and focus on his voicing. He felt nervous, worried she might receive his apology as a sign of weakness. But this felt like the right thing to do. Whether she chose to accept it or not was up to her. As she saw him approach, Deborah didn't look pleased. Allen took a deep breath. He determined to say everything that needed to be said, and to be as respectful as he could.

Allen: I'd like to apologise, Deborah.
Deborah: For what?

Allen: For being rude and disrespectful and for not listening to you.

Deborah: Go on.

Allen: (*Takes a deep breath.*) I am so focussed on delivering the numbers next year. The team, quite honestly, doesn't have much faith in how the plan numbers were arrived at, but we are all committed to doing the best we can. But to hit those numbers we believe we will need to spend. I got frustrated yesterday when you said we needed to cut our plan numbers by 30%. It felt like another kick in the guts.

Deborah: I see.

Allen: Then I called you an obstacle when I'm sure you're just doing your job, and I didn't stop to ask what's happening for you.

Deborah: No, you didn't.

Allen: That's what I'm apologising for.

Deborah: Apology accepted.

Allen: So, can we start again? Can you help me understand why I need to cut costs by 30% next year?

Deborah: Because that's what the leadership team told the Board they would deliver across the business. Because those are the numbers in the business case. If the CEO went back now and said he wanted to increase costs, he would lose all credibility.

Allen: Does that mean we all have to cut costs 30%?

Deborah: Not necessarily. But no one is putting their hands up to cut costs. Everyone would like someone else to cut costs so they can increase costs. Though only you have asked to increase your costs by as much as 30%.

Allen: Why did the leadership team promise to do that?

Deborah: Because, as I said, those are the numbers in the acquisition business case. The Board approved the deal on the basis that we would find $30 million of cost synergies.

Allen: So, we could increase costs somewhat, if we demonstrated $30 million of underlying cost savings?

Deborah: Possibly, but we'd have to make a very clear case and the leadership would have to be all onside. Right now, the leadership team is so fed up that no one recognises the importance of cutting costs, they're not in the mood to hear requests to increase costs.

Allen: So, what do I do?

Deborah: You develop your best case scenario on the basis that you cut your costs by 30%. That shows you're serious and understand what's going on. That's your start point, and you need to convince people that you've really embraced the challenge and pushed your numbers.

Allen: (*Sighing.*) We can't be the only team in this predicament. What do you think of all this?

Deborah: This is what always happens in an acquisition or merger. To get the deal across the line, people build artificially optimistic assumptions into the business case. The leadership team and the Board know that. They know it's going to be hard and they probably have some leeway built into the overall numbers that I don't know about. You want my advice?

Allen: Yes, please.

Deborah: Go talk to people. Take every opportunity to bump into members of the leadership team and the Board. Ask a lot of questions and don't tell people the numbers are unrealistic. They know that already. They're looking for people who can help us move ahead as best we can.

Go talk to people, Allen thought. That sounded like navigating power and engaging in dialogue. He straightaway began to think – who might be some of the less obvious people to start building relationships with? And how to make sure he stayed in a dialogic mindset? He gave Kelly a call and told her what happened.

Kelly and Allen discuss power

Kelly and Allen talk on the phone.

Allen: Thank you for sharing with me the materials on dialogue. I understand it, I think. I hadn't appreciated the extent to which I'm making judgements and assumptions all the time, and how that's getting in the way of relationship building. At times I feel like just holding it all in and smiling sweetly, but I don't think that would work either.

Kelly: Dialogue isn't just about listening and being nice. It's about saying what needs to be said as well. We have to be genuinely respectful, which demands high levels of self-awareness and reflection in the moment.

Allen: I understand. But I'm not sure I see dialogue as the answer to everything. For example, if I want to engage my peers in a conversation around working together differently, then I don't think everyone will truly engage. A couple of the current team feel threatened by the idea of reviewing roles and responsibilities. They are concerned about losing power and status, and that will inevitably impact on how they show up in a team meeting. They may listen and show all signs of being respectful, but they won't genuinely engage in dialogue if the topic of conversation is one that they feel threatened by. Indeed, they will do all they can behind the scenes to avoid any changes to the status quo. My talking about dialogue and trying to do dialogue myself isn't going to be enough.

Kelly: Agreed. Let's talk about power.

Allen: Deborah told me to go talk to people. Talking to the leadership team is obvious, but who else should I talk to? I spoke to Deb because she needs to be onside for the CEO to be onside. I didn't think anyone else really mattered, but she says I should take to the whole team.

Kelly: Question then would be – who needs to be onside for Deborah to be onside.

Allen: Hmm. She has half an eye on the Board. I think she has a pretty good relationship with the Chairperson, and a couple of other folks who she knows well. I think she takes her reading of the Board from them and then lets the CEO know how things are likely to land.

Kelly: And how do those three members of the Board form their opinions?

Allen: They all have relationships inside the organisation, but I don't know what relationships they have outside the organisation. I need to find out.

Kelly: How will you do that?

Allen: I'm going to go back and have another conversation with Deborah for starters. And I know two people who know the Chairperson quite well. One of them went to school with her. He manages the capital allocation committee. The other has been around for more than 25 years. He's well networked into three of our main competitors.

Kelly and Allen discuss politics

At their next session Allen told Kelly how he'd been spending his time since last they met. He'd met with both the leadership team members who believed it was their role to give Allen and his team direction. In both meetings he focussed only on trying to understand their perspectives. In listening to what they had to say, it became apparent that the members of the leadership team were finding it hard to make time to talk with each other, and that when they did make the time to talk to each other, difficult topics of conversations were being circumvented and avoided. The Marketing Director saw it as his role to provide direction, particularly with regard to online marketing strategy. The Sales Director saw the online channel predominantly as a sales channel. Allen listened hard to both their arguments and made sure he understood them. He bottled his own anxieties as to how hard it would be to respond to two different agendas, and at the same time made sure he didn't agree to anything that would further confuse him and the team. The Marketing Director became frustrated, but Allen quietly explained his position and suggested they meet together all three of them, to agree a path forward. The Marketing Director looked annoyed but didn't push back.

Allen: It's going to take time, but I get the point about networks and power. I have to find out how the land lies before we go trying to persuade people to support a particular course of action. I think the Marketing Director also has a greater appreciation of our circumstances and how challenging it will be for us if he and the Sales Director don't work together.

Kelly: Sounds good. How do you feel about it?

Allen: Like I said, it will take time. I don't think it will be easy to get the two of them together, but I'm going to try and make it as easy as possible for them. I don't think they see eye to eye. But that's not really what I want to talk about today.

Kelly: What do you want to talk about?

Allen: You were right when you said the team meeting may not have hit the mark last month. Ever since then the team has been quiet. I sense they are waiting for me to provide all the answers. I don't mind doing the hard yards with the leadership team, but I need them to build bridges with other teams. It's not an easy environment at the moment and I think they're finding it hard. I keep hearing the phrase 'I don't get involved in the politics', and it's driving me a bit nuts.

Kelly: What does 'getting involved in the politics' mean?

Allen: It seems to mean dealing with people who are untrustworthy, who don't say what they mean, whose behaviour doesn't match their words. The trouble is that the team seems to be tarring everyone with the same brush right now, and if we don't build those relationships, then life is going to be very hard long term.

Kelly: What are you thinking to do moving forward?

Allen: I'm not sure. I may have made life difficult for myself the way I managed the last meeting. I think I gave them the impression that everything is under control, when in fact nothing is under control. I think I'm going to need to spend as much time with them as I am with other stakeholders, in the first place just seeking to understand their perspectives. It's so easy to slip into solution mode, especially when busy. And if I want them to speak freely to me I'm going to have to speak freely to them.

Kelly: How will you encourage them to get energised around relationship building?

Allen: Again, role modelling, I suspect. And helping them see everyone inevitably has a different agenda. That doesn't mean people are untrustworthy and conniving. I have to manage my own frustration with people not only in relating to those people but in describing those relationships to people on my team. I need to create conversations and make sure those conversations are conducted respectfully.

Kelly: Any specifics come to mind?

Allen: First job is to get the two online distributions people talking to each other. They are already starting to put up walls. That's not going to help anyone. We need to have a conversation about what we're trying to achieve as a bigger team and draw out what people are thinking on to the table.

Kelly and Allen discuss conflict

Kelly and Allen meet for a coffee.

Allen: I'm getting a little concerned that I may be making a bit of a name for myself for being an awkward so-and-so. Can you coach me as to how I can ruffle people's feathers less and get along with everyone a bit better?

Kelly: Do you have an example?

Allen: Sure. I spoke with the Head of Strategy yesterday. I listened to what she said and it all made sense. We committed to a three-year plan two years ago and the Board expects us to follow through on it. She's personally anxious to ensure that we don't allow ourselves to be knocked off course by all the operational issues we have in bedding down the acquisition. She shared lots of stories from her previous organisation where strategy went out of the window in order to achieve short-term goals. I believe I understand where she is coming from. Even taking that into account, though, I do think the new portfolio of assets merits a new play which will not only help us in the short term but also creates a new longer term play that is totally consistent with the high-level purpose, mission, etc., we agreed three years ago.

Kelly: What happened?

Allen: She got quite angry and said I needed to trust her judgement. That now wasn't the time to be taking new projects and plans to the Board. I said I recognised it would mean some hard work in influencing some of the Board members, even assuming we get the rest of the leadership team to support the idea, but I didn't see the logic in not progressing the proposal given the potential benefits. She then just said I didn't have her support and made it clear she didn't want to carry on the conversation. Should I go apologise, do you think?

Kelly: Apologise for what?

Allen: I'm not sure. I really did make a genuine attempt to hear her, and nothing she said leads me to think I got anything wrong. True, I don't understand why she got quite so upset, but she stopped talking to me at that point. And I spoke to her respectfully. She does great work, she's smart . . . I have no criticism of her, but I was just saying what I was thinking.

Kelly: What will you apologise for then?

Allen: Again, not sure. But I don't want to be in a position where she doesn't want to talk to me. That isn't going to help me or her or the business.

Kelly: Is the next conversation an apology conversation then – or a different kind of conversation?

Allen: What do you mean?

Kelly: What happens if you apologise?

Allen: She assumes I will go along with what she wants. Which I won't.

Kelly: So, what conversation do you want to have?

Allen: I guess I want her to know that I respect her and that I want to keep on talking. I also want her to know that I appreciate being able to have a candid conversation, that I don't want to feel like I'm constantly deciding what to share with her and what to hold back. I wonder how she feels about all that, and what it would take to be able to have that sort of conversation.

Coaching through this lens

Based on a meta-systemic philosophy, we will likely witness the following behaviours in a coach:

1 **Plotting social networks**

The coach will be curious about the world in which the coachee operates, and her thinking won't be unhelpfully restrained by thoughts of systems and boundaries. That isn't to say the coach isn't perfectly happy to play with these metaphors but will do so when it seems helpful.

The coach will encourage the coachee to think in terms of social networks and power dynamics. The approach will be more sophisticated than simple stakeholder analysis. Stakeholder analysis tends to be based on hierarchy and positional power, expressed in terms of fixed boundaries, and tends to be individualistic and static. The meta-systemic coach is thinking about patterns of relationship first and foremost and is then curious as to the dynamics functioning within those networks. Power dynamics can only be hypothesised since we can never be sure of the impact of all the various forms of power. The impact of power is in any case relational, since the perception of power is subjective.

Sean O'Connor and Michael Cavanagh (more eminent coaching psychologists) have started doing some work on social network analysis in the context of coaching.[12] They coached one group of people and compared them with another group of people who didn't receive coaching. They drew up social networks based on people filling out forms to say who they communicated with, within the organisation and how often. They measured levels of wellbeing across the organisation, before, during and after coaching took place. They found that people whose wellbeing improved the most were closest to those who received coaching in the network. They also found that quality of interaction deteriorated for those closest to people being coached, an unexpected finding. This is an interesting study in that it explicitly begins to explore the impact of coaching in a context. The authors succeed in their objective, which was to provide evidence that the impact of coaching extends beyond the person being coached.

Through a meta-lens, the social network in their study seems to reflect participants' perceptions as to who they are in relationship with. If, for example, a leader speaks regularly to the man who empties the dishwasher in the canteen, he probably doesn't include those conversations in his network analysis. Nor the conversations he has with family and friends, because the methodology encourages him to think only about work interactions. There is an implicit systemic boundary showing up in the narrative.

The analysis seems to assume that participants know how often they interact with people. This may be relatively easy in a work context where people can look at their diaries to see how often they interact with others. It is less easy for less formal relationships. The interactions that stick in the mind will predominate. The conversations the leader has with the man who empties the dishwasher may be less clear. But, unbeknownst to the leader, those conversations may play a role in the co-creation of his intentions. Upon exclaiming 'Eureka!' Archimedes may have been suddenly aware that the volume of irregular objects can be measured with precision, but he would have been much less aware as to how that realisation arose, the myriad of conversations he had before that fateful day he stepped into his bath. Through a meta-lens, the coach regards social networks as dynamic and constantly evolving. The impact of the conversations the leader has within these networks is complex. The insight he comes up with on Tuesday may be the impact of a series of conversations held over a long period of time, including a short period when he engaged in conversation with that person who he no longer encounters anymore; that strange little fellow who sat quietly at the table during that one meeting we had with that client, who said only one thing, now entirely forgotten. But who knows what the impact of that conversation was on the leader's thinking?

The meta-systemic coach is likely grateful to O'Connor and Cavanagh for shifting the coaching research agenda away from a mostly first order exploration of the impact of coaching, and welcomes further exploration of the functioning of coaching in social networks, networks not always conceived in terms of systems and boundaries.

2 Focus on relationships

The meta-systemic coach, like the complexity coach, is focussed on local interaction. If change takes place through interaction, then she is curious to observe and understand more of those interactions. The meta-systemic coach is as likely as the complexity coach to be interested in interacting with other stakeholders. Like the complexity coach, she is watching carefully the nature of the interaction between coachee and others in her network, constructing hypotheses as to the functioning of the relationship and its role in the unfolding of events in the coachee's world. The complexity coach, however, may sometimes gain only a relatively narrow perspective on the functioning of the coachee's social networks. The line manager relationship may be over-privileged, because positional power is unwittingly screening the coach's attention. The meta-systemic coach is constantly curious as to how the social networks in which the coachee operates seem to be functioning. Stakeholder analysis tends to be individualistic. It is about my relationship with persons x, y and z, and how I can better manage those individual relationships. When we look at a social network through a complexity lens, we are looking at patterns of relationship. When we look through a meta-systemic lens, we are looking at a broader patter of relationships, aware that the notion of boundaries may limit our vision.

3 Engaging in dialogue

You will have noticed Kelly and Allen talking about dialogue. Dialogue is a particular type of conversation. Consider Figure 6.1, adapted from William Isaacs's book, *Dialogue and the Art of Thinking Together*.[13] This helps differentiate dialogue from other forms of conversation.

Most conversations we have are monologic, particularly when we are time-constrained (which in many

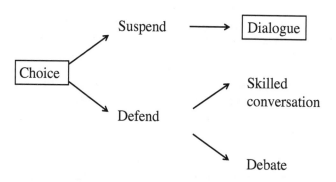

Figure 6.1 Types of conversation

organisations is all the time). Skilled conversation and debate are forms of monologue. These conversations may be perfectly effective. Skilful debate is effective in certain circumstances, for example when we want to test the underlying assumptions of a particular perspective. Skilled conversation is when people come together to share alternative perspectives in service of coming up with an agreed way forward. In essence, it is like a negotiation, with final agreements featuring a bit of my stuff, a bit of your stuff, etc. If managed skilfully, this kind of conversation can be polite and harmonious and lead to stronger relationships, but it isn't dialogue. Dialogue entails putting aside my 'noble certainties' and engaging with someone on their own terms. It means being open to whatever may eventuate. From skilled conversation is likely to emerge compromise. From dialogue may emerge something new.

At the heart of dialogue sits respect. Simply put, dialogue comprises listening and voicing. When I listen to someone with dialogic mindset, I am utterly curious. I want to completely understand what you are trying to say. This won't happen if I don't bring respect. Without respect, I will stop listening at some point, probably quite early on, and I will run with my assumptions. I am listening to understand what you are trying to say, and I am continually checking in to make sure I have understood. And I am listening to you as a person – *why* are you trying to say this? Who are you? Who am I talking to? Equally dialogue is about voicing, about saying that thing that needs to be said. But effective voicing is not the same as venting. Venting is generally a release of tension, a release of pent-up frustration with someone or something. It often involves labelling someone, judging someone. Effective voicing is again built on respect, a belief-in-the-moment that the person I'm talking to is a human being who deserves of me my complete attention and consideration.

The practice of dialogue is relevant to both the coach and the leader. When we create the space for dialogue, we create the space for a particularly rich type of conversation, one in which everyone is heard and everything is called out. Dialogue doesn't offer the leader control, but it does offer an opportunity to foster and nurture a collective sense-making process that may lead to insights and outcomes that would not have emerged otherwise. Leaders will come to understand aspects of the social network that they didn't understand before. Their capacity to influence will be enhanced. They will understand better what is on people's minds. They speak with courage, especially when things are unclear and ambiguous and volatile. They don't see it as their role always to bring certainty, and they are happy to speculate. Through dialogue they are most likely to *influence* outcomes. They know they can't *control* outcomes, and they are content with that, in the same way they are content that sometimes it rains in the morning and sometimes it doesn't.

The meta-systemic coach knows also that you don't need dialogue to happen in an organisation for things to change. Change emerges from all interaction and relating. People bring power to conversations. Moments of dialogue may be fleeting and occasional. I may be fully immersed in another person's point of view for two minutes, then suddenly experience an overwhelming desire to tell them why they are wrong such that I stop listening. Or I may be distracted by my phone flashing. Or I may simply get tired. Dialogue is not some kind of magical or mystical state that we can all descend into for hours at a time. It is a state of mind that we can encourage but not demand of others. But as a state of mind in the leader, it can be very useful in seeking to understand the nature of the social networks in which we are operating, and to influence others.

4 Exploring power

Some writers believe that pure dialogue is impossible, because, they say, dialogue can happen only in the absence of power. Power impacts the outcome of conversation. But how useful is it to think about dialogue in binary terms? Dialogue may not only be present or not present, its presence is also electric and fleeting. In 2018, seven of us sat down together for three days to talk about dialogue, from which emerged the book *The Tao of Dialogue*.[14] Upon reflection, we noticed how dialogue seemed to dance between us. Five people might be engaged in an intent process of listening, reflection and voicing, only for the 'spell' to be broken by an offhand remark by a sixth person who was at that moment out of tune with everyone else. Dialogue in this sense is about purpose and energy in the moment.

What breaks the spell? What limits the capacity of a group of people in a moment of time to engage in dialogue? Simple distraction, of course. But also, the decision of one or more people to wield power, often unwittingly. For example, a group of people are exploring how they might best manage the company's response to coronavirus. Everyone is doing their best to be open to the views of others. Everyone is expressing their perspective transparently and respectfully. Then one person says, "I don't think our key clients will tolerate that course of action. I don't think I'm prepared to test that idea with them." Everyone else nods, and the conversation moves on. What just happened? One person shifted out of enquiry mode and established a limit to where the conversation was able to progress. That doesn't mean that the group's commitment to dialogue isn't useful or productive. The meta-systemic coach is attuned to the presence and exercising of power. The social network isn't only a pattern of relationships; it is also a pattern of power dynamics, different forms of power, again always shifting and evolving and ultimately hypothetical.

5 All tools are good

Some of you may be hanging out for the section that tells you how to coach from a meta-systemic perspective. What do meta-systemic coaches do? This is the voice of the pragmatist in service of the practical. This is good. From the complexity and meta-perspectives we learn through doing and reflecting on that doing. But my answer to the question – what tools and frameworks can I use and not use as a meta-systemic coach? – is, all tools are good. The first order coach may like the GROW model and a focus on forming goals and taking actions to get nearer and nearer to those goals. Other first order coaches may like the 'five whys' as a means by which to get to the heart of an issue. The second order coach may like 'rich picturing' as technique through which to co-create a perspective on the current state of the system. The complexity coach may commend any process that entails the coach interacting with other people in the organisation. From a meta-perspective, all these tools are good, so long as we use them through the lens of metaphor.

Take constellations work as an example. John Whittington wrote a book called *Systemic Coaching and Constellations*.[15] In the book he defines systemic coaching as "that which acknowledges, illuminates and releases the system dynamics so that each element can function with ease. It is coaching that prioritises the system." He writes about the limitations of rational thinking and linear thinking. A constellation, he suggests, depicts 'natural orders', 'organizing principles' or forces that sustain systems. The first stage of a constellation is "designed to support the client to stand in the truth of the current situation". This way of thinking about systems would appear then to be closest to second order thinking. It isn't first order linear, because he says that causal relationships are more complex. It doesn't sound like first order non-linear, because he says that the functioning of the system cannot be understood only through a rational lens. Nevertheless, it sounds like a realist perspective. The system may be mysterious, but it is real, sustained by a finite number of hidden forces; time, place and exchange. The creation of a constellation is a social process, in that multiple perspectives are engaged in service of finding the 'truth'.

Let us just suppose for a moment, for the sake of argument, that the underlying philosophy behind Whittington's work is second order. This doesn't mean that others cannot derive equal value from a process that entails people mapping their system spatially. I may not go about the process in the way that Whittington suggests, but I can nevertheless learn from some of the processes he has developed how to map out a system or a social network in a way that yields useful insights for the person or people being coached. Or I may go along with both the process and the underlying philosophy, holding the philosophy lightly, again in search of insights that may prove useful.

The meta-coach is open to all practices and processes, and to holding lightly underlying philosophies, where they are apparent. Through a meta-lens, holding it all lightly as metaphor, all tools are good.

Leading through this lens

The leader looking at life through a meta-systemic lens may appear similar to the leader considering things through a complexity perspective. She has her finger on the pulse of what's happening across the organisation and how things are connected. She has a wide network of relationships and spends time with people outside her immediate area of focus. The difference may be that she spends more time outside the organisation than others. She may evidently take the idea of boundaries with a pinch of salt. The notion that the organisation is operating in silos may appear simplistic and even limiting. Whilst some people never quite get around to networking outside the organisation, this leader seems to be operating to different principles in terms of who they make time to talk to. She connects deeply with people, recognising that it is only ever through relationships that she succeeds in her role as leader. She pays attention to power dynamics, recognising other people's strengths and weaknesses through a power lens. One of her primary sources of power is relationship power. When it comes to any scenario or issue, she seems to know everyone she needs to know. If she doesn't, then she invests time in building that relationship. Faced with conflict or challenge, she doesn't respond defensively. She is curious and seeks to understand better the person issuing the challenge.

Developing leaders

Again, I'm not sure I've ever experienced a leadership programme that truly seems to have been designed according to meta-systemic principles. Such a programme would again place an emphasis on practical experience and the opportunity to reflect on that experience with others. It would focus on how people think and provide experiences in which the leader would have to seek out a different way of thinking. It would help the leader think more holistically and to appreciate the value of attuning into the functioning of social networks. It probably *wouldn't* introduce the leader to the idea of systems thinking, or if it did, it would do so whilst simultaneously encouraging the leader to hold such ideas as metaphor. The programme would focus on relationship and an awareness of power. The programme would be practical and pragmatic above all else, helping leaders to critique and review their way of looking at the world and to do so in the company of others.

At the movies

Harri Raisio and Niklas Lundström didn't suggest a movie to watch to further explore the meta-perspective, but I found interesting snippets in the book and television series *Dirk Gently's Holistic Detective Agency*.

First, the author, Douglas Adams, encourages us not to dismiss the value of first and second order thinking. If you are now feeling sceptical about the notion that the first order perspective adds any value:

> "I commend you on your scepticism, but even the sceptical mind must be prepared to accept the unacceptable when there is no alternative. If it looks like a duck, and quacks like a duck, we have at least to consider the possibility that we have a small aquatic bird of the family *Anatidæ* on our hands."

This might compel us to compare a fear of first order perspectives to anatidaephobia, or the fear of ducks. There are, however, limitations to the first order philosophy, the possibility that we may sometimes be too quick to seize upon an initial, simplistic, analysis of an issue:

> "Sherlock Holmes observed that once you have eliminated the impossible then whatever remains, however improbable, must be the answer. I, however, do not like to eliminate the impossible."

We can be quick to defend our analyses, regarding them as truth:

> "Gilks sighed. "You're a clever man, Cjelli, I grant you that," he said, "but you make the same mistake a lot of clever people do of thinking everyone else is stupid.""

Adams, via Dirk, on the Wiener Filter:

> "Don't you understand that we need to be childish in order to understand? Only a child sees things with perfect clarity, because it hasn't developed all those filters which prevent us from seeing things that we don't expect to see."

Adams also appears to recognise the underlying principles of the second order systems thinking:

> "There are some oddities in the perspective with which we see the world."

Adams, via Dirk, on the nature of sense-making:

> "What I mean is that if you really want to understand something, the best way is to try and explain it to someone else. That forces you to sort it out in your own mind. And the more slow and dim-witted your pupil, the more you have to break things down into more and more simple ideas. By the time you've sorted out a complicated idea into little steps that even a stupid machine can deal with, you've certainly learned something about it yourself. The teacher usually learns more than the pupil. Isn't that true?"

Finally, the value in looking at patterns:

> "The term 'holistic' refers to my conviction that what we are concerned with here is the fundamental interconnectedness of all things. I do not concern myself with such petty things as fingerprint powder, tell-tale pieces of pocket fluff and inane footprints. I see the solution to each problem as being detectable in the pattern and web of the whole. The

connections between causes and effects are often much more subtle and complex than we with our rough and ready understanding of the physical world might naturally suppose, Mrs Rawlinson. Let me give you an example. If you go to an acupuncturist with toothache he sticks a needle instead into your thigh. Do you know why he does that, Mrs Rawlinson? No, neither do I, Mrs Rawlinson, but we intend to find out."

Your 3Ps

1 What was useful about the theory of complex responsive processes?
2 Which is your favourite Dirk Gently quote? (And why?)
3 What sense does the meta-perspective make?
4 If you review your Purpose again now, has it changed at all? Can it be further refined?
5 Do you have a glimpse yet of what other practical approaches you might seek to integrate in your practice?

Segue . . .

Kelly and Allen have finished for the time being. They have both emerged from their time together as different people. They have accessed different ways of thinking. Kelly wants to go away and reflect on the nature of that change within herself. She decides to revisit her 3Ps . . .

Notes

1 Stacey, R.D. & Mowles, C. (2016). *Strategic Management and Organisational Dynamics*, 7th edition. Pearson.
2 Stacey, R.D. & Mowles, C. (2016). *Strategic Management and Organisational Dynamics*, 7th edition. Pearson. Page 300.
3 This was not Stacey's intention. Stacey says the original purpose of his model was to classify different decision-making techniques on the basis of assumptions they appeared to make about context [Stacey, R. (2012). Comment on debate article: Coaching Psychology Coming of Age: The Challenges We Face in the Messy World of Complexity. *International Coaching Psychology Review*, 7(1), 91–95].

4 Higgs, M. & Rowland, D. (2011). What Does It Take to Implement Change Successfully? A Study of the Behaviors of Successful Change Leaders. *Journal of Applied Behavioral Science*, *47*(3), 309–355.

5 Stacey, R.D. & Mowles, C. (2016). *Strategic Management and Organisational Dynamics*, 7th edition. Pearson. Page 287.

6 Bachkirova, T. & Borrington, S. (2020). Beautiful Ideas That Can Make Us Ill: Implications for Coaching. *Philosophy of Coaching: An International Journal*, *5*(1), 9–30.

7 Gover, L. & Duxbury, L. (2012). Organizational Faultlines: Social Identity Dynamics and Organizational Change. *Journal of Change Management*, *12*(1), 53–75.

8 Bohm, D. (1996). *On Dialogue*. Routledge. Page 49.

9 Morgan, G. (2006). *Images of Organization*. Sage.

10 Morgan lists 14 forms of power.

11 A point made by Tatiana Bachkirova in the beautifully titled Let Us Not Throw the Individual Baby Out with the Non-Systemic Bath Water, *International Coaching Psychology Review*, *7*(1), 98–100.

12 O'Connor, S. & Cavanagh, M. (2013). The Coaching Ripple Effect: The Effects of Developmental Coaching on Wellbeing across Organisational Networks. *Psychology of Well-Being: Theory, Research and Practice*, *3*(2), 1–23.

13 Isaacs, W. (1999). *Dialogue and the Art of Thinking Together*. Currency & Doubleday.

14 Lawrence, P., Hill, S., Priestland, A., Forrestal, C., Rommerts, F., Hyslop, I. & Manning, M. (2019). *The Tao of Dialogue*. Routledge.

15 Whittington, J. (2012). *Systemic Coaching and Constellations: An Introduction to the Principles, Practices and Application*. Kogan Page.

7

Becoming more systemic

The premise of this book is that you are already systemic. To be a systemic coach means nothing more than looking more broadly at the work that you do. We are nevertheless exhorted to be *more* systemic. That usually means being more systemic with reference to a particular philosophy or in the sense of adopting a particular methodology. People have started to define what it means to be systemic in their own terms, and to exclude some versions of systemic on the basis they are not systemic enough. For example, the distinction between systemic and systematic, which basically means excluding first order thinking.

In this book, to be more systemic means to have access to new ways of thinking, to have a broader frame of reference and to have integrated those new ways of thinking into your practice. If we are not interested in accessing new ways of thinking, then how likely are we to be successful in encouraging our clients to consider new ways of thinking? To what extent will we be fit for purpose in helping our clients think through complexity? In seeking to become systemic, we need to look beyond the first theory or framework we come across. There is a difference between latching onto bite-size pieces of theory and advocating these isolated chunks of understanding as something fundamentally different, and taking the time to scan the field, to understand it and to come up with your own thoughtful articulation of what it means to you to be systemic.

The framework around which this book is structured is not a menu from which to make a single selection. It

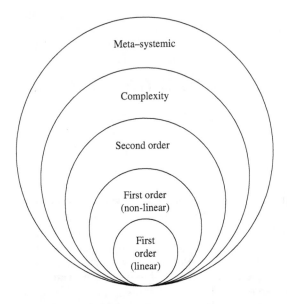

Figure 7.1 Five ways of thinking about systems

represents five categories of systems thinking that have emerged in the literature roughly in this order (Figure 7.1).

Revisiting your 3Ps

The scallop model in Figure 7.1 is my attempt to make sense of a vast literature on systems thinking. I don't expect it to make complete sense to you. Some aspects of it may resonate and other aspects may not. I will not be at all put out if no one likes it very much. Indeed, I encourage you to build your own models and frameworks that better represent your personal perspective on systems thinking. As the world continues to evolve, so must we as coaches.

The 3Ps model is a simple, neat framework we can use to track our development, to stay focussed and aware on who we are as coaches today and who we seek to become. It helps us to continually challenge ourselves: Do the theories I espouse manifest in my practice? To fundamentally change the way we think and behave starts with an examination of how we currently think and behave. As Arnold Beisser put it more than 50 years ago:[1]

> change occurs when one becomes what he is, not when he tries to become what he is not. Change does not take place through a coercive attempt by the individual or by another person to change him, but it does take place if one takes the time and effort to be what he is – to be fully invested in his current positions.

The 3Ps model is a framework for reflecting on our 'current position'. The first step in seeking to become more systemic then is to ask ourselves now, what do we mean by systemic? What theories and frameworks appeal to us, and how do these models manifest themselves in our coaching? To help you, let us now review some of the materials we have covered. As you read through this summary, ask yourself what sticks, what interests you and what you reject. Now is a good time to revisit what you wrote in Chapter 1 and refer to any notes you may have written in reading this book.

First, let us revise first order linear thinking (Table 7.1). Leading through this lens is about designing the system, focussing on both task and motivating people, and seeking feedback to see how I personally need to adapt my behaviour to be most effective. The coach thinks in terms of generic leadership competencies and sees their role as helping clients come up with goals and actions to achieve those goals. The organisation is a system, a machine.

The non-linear first order perspective is still first order in that it still regards the organisation as a real system whose functioning can be analysed and understood (Table 7.2). The leader still assumes a dual role, stepping outside the system to redesign it, and then back inside to play her role as a cog in the wheel. The main difference between linear and non-linear perspectives is that the leader recognises that relationships between different parts of the system are sometimes complex and difficult to discern. The leader is less likely to come to quick conclusions, and the coach is more likely to slow things down to poke and prod the leaders' thinking.

Table 7.1 First order linear thinking

Philosophy	Purpose	Practice
Scientific management and a focus on task.	Helping the coachee to have an immediate impact on the organisation through exercising the coachee's individual 'greatness'.	Looking through the Wiener Filter to identify simple root cause and effect.
Mayo's work pinpointing the importance of motivation.		Focus on goals and actions.
Norbert Wiener, cybernetics, and the Wiener Filter.		Talking about boundaries as if real.
Simple, linear, cause and effect	Changing an organisation one person at a time.	Change as a programme or project, with beginning, middle and end.
Organisation as system, as machine.	Helping the organisation to develop great leaders.	
People as cogs in the wheel.		Focus on the individual.
The powerful leader doing change to the organisation.		

Table 7.2 First order non-linear thinking

Philosophy	Purpose	Practice
Senge's work on systems dynamics – causal loops and non-linear causal relationships.	Helping the coachee to have an immediate impact on the organisation through exercising the coachee's individual 'greatness' and solving complicated problems.	Asking the 'five whys' to get to the bottom of issues.
Living systems theory – organisation as a living organism.		Organisation as systems and sub-systems.
Organisation as system, as machine.		Thinking of environment in terms of sub-systems, e.g. PESTLE.
People as cogs in the wheel.	Changing an organisation one person at a time.	Change as a programme or project, with beginning, middle and end.
The powerful leader doing change to the organisation.	Helping the organisation to develop great leaders.	Focus on the individual.

The second order perspective still regards the organisation as a real system (Table 7.3), but the system is mysterious, and no one can assume that their *perspective* of the system is real. In effect, the organisation-as-a-system is always a hypothesis. The emphasis is on learning through doing – learning about the system as well as learning how to address a particular issue. The leader still assumes a dual role, stepping outside the system to redesign it, and then back inside to play her role as a cog in the wheel. The leader recognises the shortcomings of their individual perception and seeks others' perspectives as a matter of course. The coach encourages the leader to explore others' perspectives and to integrate some of those perspectives into his own.

The complexity perspective still regards the organisation as a system (Table 7.4), but the system works differently than envisaged by first and second order ways of thinking. Change at the macro level emerges from interactions at the micro level. The leader cannot control outcomes, but he can

Table 7.3 Second order thinking

Philosophy	Purpose	Practice
We are all frogs. Our perceptions are all subjective, determined by our mental models.	Encouraging the coachee to seek out others' perspectives and understand their mental models.	Organisation as systems and sub-systems.
Checkland and Soft Systems Methodology.	To engage with others in collective problem solving.	Holding our perspective of events lightly.
The organisation is a system, whose functioning is dark and mysterious.	Changing an organisation one person at a time.	Seeking multiple perspectives.
People as cogs in the wheel.	Helping the organisation to develop great leaders.	Rich picturing.
The powerful (and collaborative) leader doing change to the organisation.		Looking through the lens of other people's mental models – ladder of inference.

Table 7.4 Complexity thinking

Philosophy	Purpose	Practice
Chaos theory	Adding value to the whole.	Looking for patterns at the macro level.
- Finding order in disorder	To help the organisation is to help everyone in the organisation. Everyone's needs are intertwined, each constantly impacting on the other	Exploring what's happening at the micro level.
- Unpredictable predictability		Experiencing the system.
The Seagull (Butterfly) Effect		Approaching conflict.
Complex adaptive systems		Understanding self in the context of the system.
- The macro and the micro		
- Everyone is always part of the system		
- Strange attractors – shifting patterns		
Change emerges.		
There exist multiple sources of power.		

influence. The leader looks for patterns of relationships and the impact of multiple sources of power on those relationships. The coach is keen to experience the system. Both leader and coach are attracted by conflict. Conflict represents a coming together of multiple perspectives and represents the possibility of innovation and purposeful change. The coach recognises they are a part of the system.

The meta-systemic perspective does not regard the organisation as a system or a sub-system (Table 7.5). The 'organisation' is regarded as a story, a simplified construct. When we talk about organisations, we are talking about patterns of relationship within a broader social system. It may be useful sometimes to talk about the organisation as if it is a system, but there are other times when the metaphor is less useful.

We also looked at team coaching through the five lenses. Perspectives on team shift significantly as you dance from

Table 7.5   Meta-systemic thinking

Philosophy	Purpose	Practice
"All anyone can ever do, no matter how powerful, is engage intentionally, and as skilfully as possible, in local interaction."	Raising people's collective awareness of the functioning of the networks within which they operate, in service of behaving more purposefully and effectively within those networks.	Plotting social networks. Focus on patterns of relationship. Appreciation of dialogue. Exploring power. All tools are good.
Every conversation that takes place within networks has potential significance.		
Organisations are stories. Organisations are not systems.		
Meaning making is social.		
Politics is.		

lens to lens. First order perspectives regard the team as a sub-system within the broader organisational system. In effect, it is a little machine of itself. To work effectively, each component must be properly programmed so that it understands its role and objectives. Through a second order lens, the machine is mysterious, the picture of its functioning fuzzy and blurred. People on the team must engage effectively, such that interpersonal dynamics become important. From a complexity perspective, interpersonal dynamics become more important, both in service of understanding how the team is functioning (and how to improve its functioning if necessary) and understanding how the team is effectively functioning within the broader social system. Through a meta-systemic lens, there is no team. Team is a construct we apply in an attempt to place a boundary between the functioning of a particular group of people and others outside that group. The task of the team coach is to hold the mirror up to a group of people the functioning of the broader social network.

So, what impact has this all had on your 3Ps? Here are just a few questions that may be useful.

Philosophy

- What is your philosophy of change?
- Whose change frameworks and models do you like?
- Do you find it useful to compare organisations to systems? If so – which kinds of system? Hot water systems, aircraft engines, living systems?
- If complexity theories form part of your philosophy, how do they sit happily alongside first and second order approaches?
- Are you afraid of ducks?
- What do you think of models such as the Stacey Model?
- What is team coaching?
- What does it mean to be a systemic coach?

Purpose

- What is your purpose?
- How do you know you are doing a good job?
- Who do you most like working with? Why?
- Who do you not like working with? Why?
- What would you like people to write on your coaching tombstone?

Practice

- How do you bring your systemic thinking to life with your client? Do you have specific techniques or stories?
- What do you do when clients demand simple answers of you?
- What do you do if your coachee reports being in conflict?
- What do you say to a coachee who expresses disgust at getting involved in office politics?
- What do you think of the GROW model?
- When coaching individuals, what questions do you ask the person briefing you? Why those questions?
- Do you conduct 360 interviews as part of coaching? If so, how do you use 360s? How do you *not* use 360s?

Once you've come up with your 3Ps, then consider sharing them with a colleague or group of colleagues and seeking feedback. Craft questions that will enable you to receive meaningful feedback from your coachees – is this the coach they experience? Practice coaching in supervision and get feedback. Reflect on your model at the end of every session, or every day, or once a week. To what extent does your practice reflect your model?

Supervision

Supervision is important if you aspire to enhance your capacity to work effectively in a complex environment. There is evidence to suggest coaching supervision is becoming more popular in many places, less so in others.[2] In the USA, for example, coach mentoring appears to be more popular. This may be in part because use of the term 'supervision' in the USA has legal implications. It may be because the ICF, as a global coaching association based in the USA, with aspirations for coaching to become formally recognised as a profession, is keen to position coaching as essentially transactional so that it can clearly differentiate coaching from therapy and psychology. And it may simply be that the words 'mentoring' and 'supervision' mean different things to different people living in different places in the world. When I say supervision is important, I am defining 'supervision' essentially as 'reflective practice'. If the word supervision offends thee, cut it out and replace it with whatever word works for you.

There are many forms of supervision. You can find a trusted colleague and meet with them on a regular basis. You might meet with a group of colleagues. You might pay someone to supervise you individually or in a group. These are all potentially useful. Each form of supervision brings with it its own challenges. Peer supervision with colleagues can turn into a 'bit of a chat' without a committed effort to conduct conversations within an agreed structure. Group supervision works well for surfacing diversities of perspective, but participants may be reluctant to share personal concerns. Individual paid supervision provides a forum for personal disclosure but doesn't offer the same diversity of perspective.

Coaching supervision is new in many places around the world. Some people take to supervision straightaway, others report feeling initially disappointed with their experience. When people feel disappointed, it is because the experience didn't meet their expectations. The solution to this is to be as purposeful as you can be about what you want from supervision. What *do* you want? Some people go to supervision to learn vicariously from others. Some people go because they want as much airtime as possible working on their own issues. Some people go for a sense of emotional connection and support. Others go because they expect the supervisor to evaluate their practice, to tell them what they are doing well and what they could be doing better. Some people go because they want to grow their businesses and are hoping to get advice from others in that regard. Most go for a mix of some or all of these reasons.

In a recent piece of research, I talked to seven group supervisors and 56 coaches being supervised.[3] Most of the supervisors said their thinking was influenced by systems thinking theories. However, the systemic lens wasn't obvious in talking to the coaches about their experience of supervision. Talking to the supervisors again, it seemed to me there were two reasons for this:

1 Some of the supervisors wanted to go where the coaches led them. If the coaches didn't lead them toward a systemic consideration of the issue at hand, then they didn't go there.
2 It wasn't clear in detail (largely because I didn't pursue the point) what specific knowledge base each supervisor was referring to.

This again helps us understand the importance of thinking purposefully about what we want to gain from supervision. If we are looking for a supervisor to help us to explore and further reflect upon our systemic stance as coach, then we need to make explicit our intention. If seeking group supervision, we may want to enquire the extent to which other participants have similar interests to us. We may want to request that the supervisor ask us questions through a systemic lens. We may want to make clear the extent to which we want to learn new theory (and how we want to learn it) versus reflecting on an existing philosophy. We may want to enquire of the supervisor their own 3Ps, and the extent to which systemic practice features in that model. We don't go the car showroom and ask the sales guy for a car. We lay out our needs in more detail. We need to do the same when seeking supervision.

If supervision is reflective practice, then we need to get out there and do the work so we can reflect on it. Doing the work is likely the only way we can truly integrate new ways of thinking. There are parallels between systems thinking and adult development theory. Both are to do with how we think. We tend to search for different ways of thinking when current ways of thinking aren't working for us.[4] Therefore, if we want to access new ways of thinking, we need to venture outside our comfort zone and just do stuff. Not so far that we fall off a cliff, but far enough to stretch the way that we think. Our supervisor is a partner on that journey.

Notes

1 Beisser, A. (1970). The Paradoxical Theory of Change. In J. Fagan & I.L Shepherd (Eds.), *Gestalt Therapy Now*. Harper & Row.
2 Hawkins, P. & Turner, E. (2017). The Rise of Coaching Supervision 2006–2014. *Coaching: An International Journal of Theory, Research and Practice*, *10*(2), 102–114.
3 Lawrence, P. (2019). What Happens in Group Supervision? Exploring Current Practice in Australia. *International Journal of Evidence Based Coaching and Mentoring*, *17*(2), 138–157.
4 Berger, J.G. (2013). *Changing on the Job: Developing Leaders for a Complex World*. Stanford University Press.

Parting comments

Gregory Bateson didn't think much of Man's ability to get things done. Purposeful, pragmatic action usually results in disaster, he said, because Man constantly overestimates his capacity to understand the world around him.

What role are we coaches playing in this? We are not neutral. Insofar as we are invited to work with people attempting to address some of the big issues we face in the world today, we are co-creators of that process and co-owners of the outcomes. That doesn't mean it is our role to tell leaders what they should be doing. That would be arrogant in the extreme. Our role, I would argue, is to help people think things through, to act as a sounding board. In acting as a sounding board, it may behove us to think not only about what is being thought about, but the nature of the thought process. If that *is* our role, then what kind of sounding board are you?

Our role includes asking questions. From what consciousness do these questions emerge? Do we want to ask questions that enable our coachees to enable access to different ways of thinking, different frames and perspectives? Or do we want our questions to remain locked within specific narrow paradigms? Our role includes challenge. Not challenge as in contradicting, dismissing or disrespecting, but challenge in the sense of bringing to the conversation a different way of looking at things, a way of looking at things that may prove useful.

Many of the people we work with have big responsibilities. People look to them for guidance when uncertain. People demand they be decisive. But the people we work with are human. They experience anxiety and stress. They function as participants in a big, complex social network, a dynamic network of interacting thoughts and emotions, swirling in patterns they often do not understand. Amidst all of this, they seek the essence of an issue. They seek to make the complex simple so they can make a decision and move on. And, according to Bateson, they don't always make a good job of it. Because the issues they are working with are *so* complex.

If our role is to facilitate thinking, asking questions and challenging along the way, then how can we be most useful? How can we do our best not to make things worse, avoid supporting leaders in making poor decisions based on simplistic perspectives? Does the way we have been taught to coach best position us to be useful? We talk a lot about goals. We have philosophies and models that encourage us to move quickly to action. Do they serve us well?

In this book I have argued that it is almost our duty to challenge our own thinking, as part of our role as coach. Don't take my exhortations too seriously. Hold them lightly. It would be paradoxical and a bit silly were I to conclude with a definitive perspective of the world today and the role we coaches should be playing. This would be a pretty good example, I think, of one man overestimating his capacity to understand the world around him. Instead, it has been my intention to stimulate thought and conversation. To encourage us all to wrap our little brains around the challenges we as coaches face, in the hope that a lot of little brains working together will function better than a lot of little brains thinking apart. Rather than gather around like a knot of frogs, all blinkered by the same inability to see what we can't see, let us be frogs who together are determined to see that which we can't see yet. And to help our clients catch a glimpse too of what might lie beyond our current line of sight.

Please feel free to dispute anything in this book. But please consider also your motivation for disputing. Are you fighting to defend a dearly held view, or are you seeking to hold forth that which might not yet be visible to myself and others? The former I think we have enough of already. The latter sounds interesting.

Appendix – 3Ps worksheet

You may find this worksheet useful is working through Chapter 1 – You as Coach.

Philosophy

What theories, model and frameworks especially appeal to you? (Choose the few that you hold most dear)

-
-
-
-
-

Why do these particular theories, models and frameworks appeal to you?

Purpose

Why do you coach? (It may be helpful to think about your past experiences and values and beliefs)

Practice

What would a fly on the wall see you doing? Think about what you do before an assignment, during a session, in between sessions, and in terms of engaging other stakeholders, for example.

Index